THE AI STOCK INVESTOR

A Beginner's Guide to Profiting from the AI Revolution

Freeman Publications

TABLE OF CONTENTS

Introduction 10

1. Demystifying AI - It's not Rocket Science, or is It? 15
So, what is AI in the first place? 15
What are the stages of AI development? 17
Weak vs. Strong AI 18
Show me the numbers 19
Applications of AI in business 20

2. Machine Learning - Teaching Elephants to Dance the New Steps . 22
What is machine learning? 23
Why do we want machines to learn? 24
Schooling the machines - how does machine learning work? 25
Machine learning trends to watch out for 28

3. Generative AI - when Machines Tell Stories 31
First things first – what's generative AI? 33
Generative AI vs. Discriminative AI 35
How does generative AI work? 36
Use cases of generative AI 38

4. Investing in Megatrends 41
Making sense of megatrends 42
3 major recent megatrends - learning from the history 44
Why AI is a megatrend to watch out for 47

5. Isaac Newton, Tulips, and Marijuana 50
Exploring market bubbles - how do they form? 52
3 of the biggest market bubbles in history 55
Avoiding the FOMO trap while investing in AI 59

6. Stages of Technology Adoption 61
Technology adoption curve 63
Factors affecting the rate of technology adoption 66

7. The Two Key AI Investing Themes - Hardware and Software..... 68
The race for futuristic hardware and software..... 69
Leading AI hardware companies 71
Leading AI software companies..... 72
8. 7 Stocks for the AI Revolution..... 75
Amazon: A Long-Term Story 75
Google: Dive Into The Dip..... 81
Intel: Take Advantage Of Near-Term Headwinds 85
Meta Platforms: Social Media Weds Artificial Intelligence 91
Microsoft: Pure AI Power 96
Nvidia: The Headwinds Are Now A Breeze..... 102
Perion Network: In A New Orbit Now 107
What about X/Y/Z stock?! 112
9. 4 AI Stocks to Avoid..... 114
10. Can AI Help You Beat the Stock Market?..... 121
Algorithmic trading, automated trading, and high-frequency trading..... 123
11. Are AI Companies Immune to Inflation? 129
Inflation, inflation everywhere 130
The potential cost of inflation to the AI Industry..... 133
12. Finding a Balance..... 138
Challenges in regulating AI 140
Potential implications of AI regulations 141
13. Conclusion 144
14. Using AI tools to Speed up Your Investing Research..... 146
Industry Overviews..... 146
Economic moats 148
Reverse thesis..... 149
Ask Your PDF 151
15. Acknowledgements 154
16. References 156

HOW TO GET THE MOST OUT OF THIS BOOK

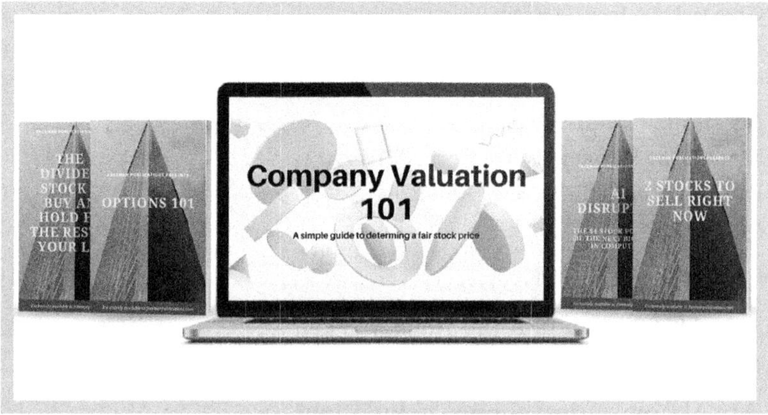

To help you along your investing journey, we've created a free bonus companion course that includes spreadsheets, bonus video content, and additional resources that will help you get the best possible results. We highly recommend you sign up now to get the most out of this book. You can do that by going to the link below or scanning the QR code with your cell phone

https://freemanpublications.com/bonus

Or text the word BONUS to 844-968-4152 (US only)

Free bonus #1: Company Valuation 101 video course ($97 value)

In this 8 part video course, you'll discover our process for accurately valuing a company. This will help you determine if a stock is overvalued, correctly valued, or a bargain. Giving you an indicator of whether to buy or not.

Free bonus #2: Guru Portfolios Analyzed ($37 value)

In these videos, we analyze the stock portfolios of Billionaire investors like Warren Buffett. As well as top entrepreneurs like Bill Gates.

Free bonus #3: Crypto 101 ($47 value)

When you have a paradigm-shifting technology like cryptocurrency and blockchain ... there are multiple ways to profit from it.

But before you rush out and buy every altcoin under the sun... there is a smarter way of doing this.

The ways used by hedge funds and Billionaire investors to make massive profits from the price of Bitcoin and other cryptocurrencies.

And you don't need anything more than a regular brokerage account to do so.

We covered exactly how to do this in a private call for our premium members recently and you'll get access to this video for free.

Free bonus #4: 2 Stocks to Sell Right Now ($17 value)

These 2 stocks are in danger of plummeting in the next 12 months. They're both popular with retail investors, and one is even in the top 5 most held stocks on Robinhood. Believe us; you don't want to be holding these going into 2021 and beyond.

Free bonus #5: AI Disruptor - The $4 Stock Poised to be the Next Big Thing in Computing ($17 value)

This under the radar company, which less than 1% of investors have heard of, is at the forefront of a breakthrough technology that will change our lives as we know them. Soon this technology will be in every smartphone, tablet, and laptop on the planet.

Free bonus #6: Options 101 ($17 Value)

Options don't have to be risky. In fact, they were invented to *reduce* risk. It's no wonder that smart investors like Warren Buffett regularly use options to supplement their long-term portfolio. In this quick start guide, we show you how options work and why they are tools to be utilized rather than feared.

Free bonus #7: The 1 Dividend Stock to Buy and Hold for the Rest of Your Life ($17 Value)

Dividends are the lifeblood of any income investor, and this stock is a cornerstone of any dividend strategy. A true dividend aristocrat with consistent payouts for over 50 years which you'll want to add to your portfolio for sure.

Free bonus #8: All the images inside this book in color ($17 Value)

As much as we'd like to print these books in full color, the printing costs prohibit us from doing so. So on our website, you can get all the images from the book in full color.

Free bonus #9: Our #1 High Yield Stock for 2023 ($17 Value)

A company with a virtual monopoly in its industry. The stock pays a 10% yield while offering capital appreciation. Best of all? It's only $9/ share.

All of these bonuses are 100% free, with no strings attached. You don't need to enter any details except your email address.

To get your bonuses go to

https://freemanpublications.com/bonus

Or text the word BONUS to 844-968-4152 (US only)

INTRODUCTION

In 1999, at the height of the dot-com boom, the legendary Venture Capitalist John Doerr referred to the internet as "the largest legal creation of wealth in human history". To say this was one of the best financial predictions ever is an understatement. Doerr was an early investor in household names like Amazon, Google and Intuit. Investments which propelled him to a net worth of over $10 Billion. It wasn't just Doerr, anyone who invested when those companies were public achieved lifechanging returns as well. $1,000 invested in Amazon's IPO would be worth roughly $1.1 million today. On a larger level, a 2021 Harvard Business School study found the internet economy was still growing 7x faster than the overall US economy.

The reason for this incredible wealth creation was the birth of what engineer and space-tech entrepreneur Peter Diamandis calls an "exponential technology". This is a technology which improves in speed while simultaneously diminishing in cost. Exponential technologies gave us the ability to order books from our phones with free overnight shipping, or read them on small handheld devices called Kindles, and allowed us to have the entire library of Alexandria in our pocket accessible 24/7/365.

Artificial Intelligence (AI) is the latest exponential technology upon us. AI is not brand new in the sense that we've seen it used in limited capacity over the past 25 years. Computers have been reading zip codes from letters since 1995. In 1997, Deep Blue, an AI-powered chess robot defeated then World Champion Gary Kasparov. In more recent times the rise of smart speakers like Amazon Alexa and Google Home have brought AI into our everyday lives.

However on November 30th 2022, everything changed. A widespread application of AI became accessible to the public, for free, in form of Open AI's ChatGPT. An AI powered chatbot which uses a large language model to answer questions, summarize long documents, debug code and even write poetry. Here are a couple of examples of ChatGPT's prowess.

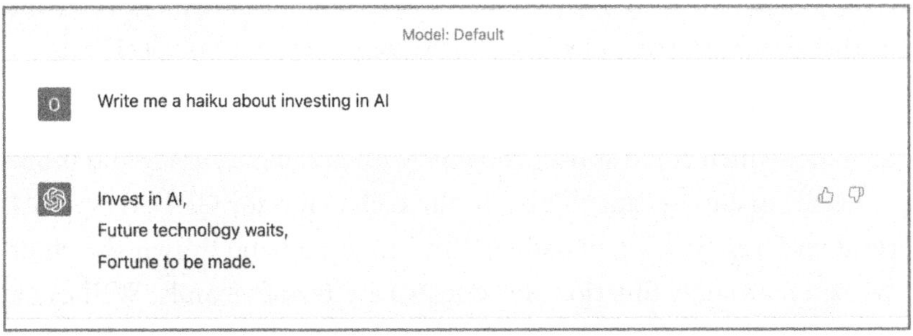

Figure 1: *ChatGPT's answer to a simple prompt (Source: ChatGPT)*

Let's try something a bit more difficult. A summary of a 640 page investing book, but written in a way that a child could understand.

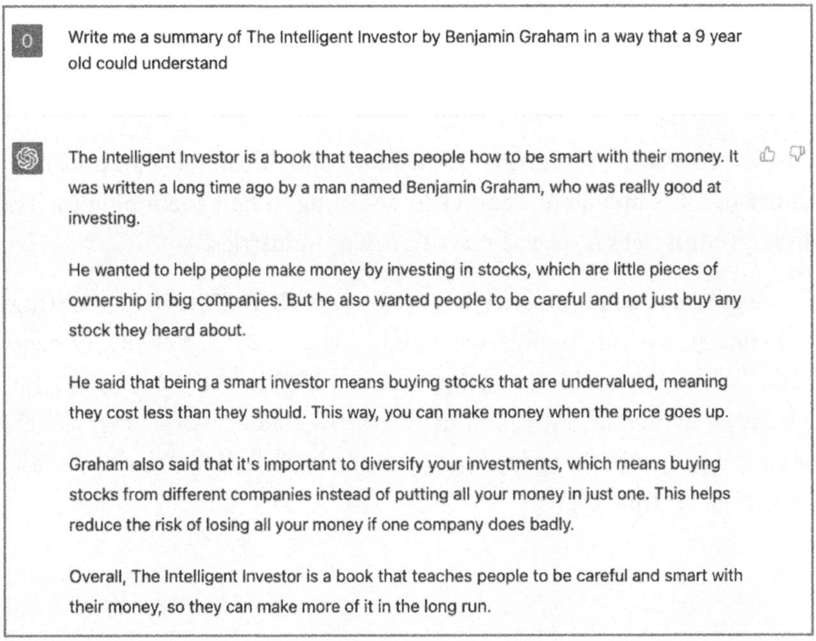

Figure 2: *ChatGPT's answer to a more complex prompt (Source: ChatGPT)*

To say ChatGPT went viral is an understatement. The tool went from 0 to 1 million users in just 5 days. For context, it took Netflix 3.5 years, AirBNB 2.5 years and Facebook 10 months to achieve the same feat. Within 2 months ChatGPT had over 100 million users averaging 13 million active users per day. Stories emerged of ChatGPT passing university entrance exams, and writing legal briefs. The tool isn't perfect, in fact just yesterday it failed a basic math problem I gave it, but it is the first mainstream use-case of AI, or generative AI specifically.

Then on March 13th, 2023, OpenAI released GPT-4. A newer version of the model which could solve problems with greater accuracy and more advanced reasoning capabilities. In the tech demo for GPT-4, OpenAI President Greg Brockman had GPT-4 convert a hand drawn sketch of a website, into fully functioning code in a matter of seconds. Without a doubt one of the most staggering demonstrations of technology I've ever seen. GPT-4 is already being used by large corporations like Morgan Stanley, Duolingo and Stripe, as well as government institutions and non-profits.

So now we know that AI is here to stay, surely investing in publicly traded AI companies is a slam-dunk way to make money fast... right? Unfortunately, it's not that easy.

You see, investors, both institutional and individual, have an uncanny ability to mess up when it comes to investing in new technologies. To highlight this, let's look at 2 recent growth industries.

The legal marijuana industry is booming, with 2022 revenues hitting $32 Billion, roughly double what they were in 2019. Yet the average publicly listed cannabis company is down 87% in the past 5 years (as measured by the largest cannabis ETF). Big names like Tilray, which once boasted a market cap of more than $100 Billion are down 98% from their all time highs.

In more recent times, we only have to look at the surge in publicly-listed Electric Vehicle companies. In 2020 alone, 22 EV companies went public, and then 2021 saw truck manufacturer Rivian debut on the Nasdaq with a higher market cap than Ford... despite never having delivered a single vehicle. In total, investors have plowed over $123 billion in these EV startups through public offerings, reverse-merger deals and other funding mechanisms in the past three years, according to Dealogic. And yet the average EV stock is down 29% since the beginning of 2021 (as measured by the Kraneshares Electric Vehicle ETF), with companies like Rivian, Nikola and Lordstown Motors down more than 80% from their peak prices.

So what is causing this? Why are individual investors losing out on these megatrends which are changing the way we live?

The way I look at it, it boils down to 2 very basic concepts. The first is simply buying stock in companies you don't understand. This is the cardinal sin of investing. Look, we've all done it. You hear about a company which is going to revolutionize an industry, how this company is a surefire winner and the stock has 100X upside from here... and you frantically open your brokerage account to hit the buy button. 6 months later the stock is down 50%, you've got no idea why, and so you sell it to move on to bigger and better opportunities. To combat this, we'll spend the first part of the book exploring the various aspects of AI and Machine Learning, as well as the fundamentals of how companies are using this technology. This is so you can at least have a basic understanding of how AI works and can look at a company to see if their AI-usage is legitimate or merely a gimmick or buzzword.

The second factor which leads to inferior investing results is the bubble-like behavior that is present in all growth industries. Humans are flawed creatures and the herd mentality which served us so well for hundreds of thousands of years, hurts us in the stock market. So we'll be addressing this in the second part of the book, and giving you the tools to not fall into the common traps which plague investors. We'll also be discussing some companies that we believe are in the best position to benefit from this megatrend, as well as some red flags and companies to avoid.

Let's also talk about what this book is not. This isn't an all-encompassing technical guide to AI, machine learning or large-language models. We'll be covering the essentials, but this isn't a textbook and was never intended to be one. This also isn't a sociopolitical musing on the long-term societal effects of AI. Nor is it a quasi-science fiction take on when the robots will become sentient and decide they no longer need us humans. One more thing, we focus solely on publicly traded companies, not private markets or angel investing.

Freeman Publications is dedicated to serving the individual investor, and our mission is to ensure regular investors get better returns in the stock market. Hence why this book, and all our books have that as our North Star goal. Since 2020 we've published 12 books, including multiple bestsellers and helped over 120,000 investors - not bad for a self-funded operation with zero help from traditional publishers.

One final word before we begin, if you're familiar with AI and ChatGPT you might be wondering - was the book written by AI? As much as that would make my life a lot easier, our books are still written, edited and proofread by actual humans.

So get comfy, grab a beverage of your choice, and let's dive into the fast moving world of AI.

Oliver El-Gorr

Founder & CEO, Freeman Publications

London, England

April 2023

Chapter 1

DEMYSTIFYING AI - IT'S NOT ROCKET SCIENCE, OR IS IT?

Those who can imagine anything can create the impossible.
- Alan Turing

In 1950, Alan Turing, widely considered the 'father of computer science', famously asked, "Can machines think?." 47 years later, IBM's chess-playing computer Deep Blue beat the then world chess champion Garry Kasparov in a chess match!

Fast forward to 2023 - you can get a sick note written by ChatGPT, ask Cortana to mail it to your boss while commanding Alexa to play Hotel California. These tools are the modern-day genies powered by *Artificial Intelligence (AI)* to carry out your commands.

The future is already here and AI is making it all possible.

So, what is AI in the first place?

Thousands of years before the arrival of modern computers, people in ancient Greece conceived the idea of thinking machines and artificial lifelike creatures. Machines with human-like intelligence have been subjects of science fiction for decades. Advancements in computing have made these myths and fiction a reality - almost.

The term 'Artificial Intelligence' was first coined by American computer scientist John McCarthy in 1955. McCarthy used this term to denote *the science and engineering of making intelligent machines, especially intelligent computer programs.* In the last 7 decades, AI has evolved to create a set of technologies that makes a computer perform work typically requiring human intelligence.

To define AI in simple words: It's a branch of computer science working on building intelligent machines that can think and function like human beings. AI is striving to build machines that simulate human intelligence. For example, an AI-assisted self-driving car can potentially drive with at least the same efficiency as an average human driver. Such autonomous cars can even exceed the performance level of human drivers by eliminating the chances of human errors. Similarly, a digital assistant like Amazon's Alexa can process natural languages and carry out different day-to-day tasks.

And, how does AI do it?

In basic forms, AI systems combine advanced computing and large datasets to create magic - computer models that can potentially 'think' and 'act' like human beings. These systems are trained on voluminous data to look for patterns and correlations and predict a future state - for say a recommended shopping list prepared based on your past purchases. Advanced AI systems apply knowledge from multiple specialized disciplines - computer science, statistics, data analytics, software engineering, neuroscience, economics, psychology, and even moral philosophy.

An AI-enabled system like Siri on your iPhone can interpret your voice commands and perform the required tasks. Using AI, computers can perform advanced functions like recommending shows on Netflix based on your past watch history or creating a playlist for you on Spotify after mapping your frequently played songs. AI systems can drive autonomous cars, detect and prevent digital frauds, work as virtual assistants, recognize faces, or even detect cancer cells.

What are the stages of AI development?

The ultimate goal of AI is to build machines possessing intelligence indistinguishable from human intelligence or even surpassing it. However, we can achieve such an ambitious goal only in stages.

These are the 4 stages of AI development:

Reactive AI

This is the first stage of AI development in which a machine can only carry out specific tasks based on certain programmed rules. These machines have limited intelligence. Also, they don't have memories to compare past actions with or to. IBM's Deep Blue, programmed to play chess, is an example of Reactive AI.

Limited memory AI

This is the current stage of AI development. At the limited memory stage, an AI system has a memory to learn from past mistakes and improve over time through training. For example, an AI system designed to detect cat pictures can be improved by training it with more and more cat pictures of different colors, shapes, and sizes. A self-driving car is another example of limited-memory AI. This autonomous system can improve over time as more data is fed into it.

Theory of mind AI

In psychology, the *theory of mind* says human beings have thoughts, feelings, and emotions necessary for social interactions. At the *theory of mind* stage of AI development, we focus on creating machines that have the social intelligence to express and understand human emotions. AI systems at this stage can emulate the human mind, make decisions like human beings and interact in a social environment. Currently, the *theory of mind* is in the conceptual stage.

Self-aware AI

Also known as AGI (Artificial General Intelligence), this is the mythical stage of AI, most commonly conceived in science fiction, in which a machine has an awareness of its existence. Such a machine can intellectualize, think like human beings, and have consciousness.

Is it possible to build such a machine that has consciousness? In 2022, a Google engineer claimed that a chatbot (a computer program that can simulate human-like conversations) had gone sentient - a claim that was promptly denied by the company.

What are the ethical repercussions of such self-aware machines? What if such a system goes rogue, like HAL in the movie 2001: A Space Odyssey? Let philosophers debate that.

Weak vs. Strong AI

An AI system can be strong or weak depending on its ability to perform various functions.

Weak AI

A *weak AI* can only perform a specific task it's designed for. *Weak AI* is also called *Narrow AI* or *Artificial Narrow Intelligence (ANI)*. A *weak AI* system cannot learn from historical transactions as it doesn't have a memory. Also, it cannot function in an unknown situation or solve a new problem.

Current AI applications are mostly *weak AI*. An example of a *weak AI* is a chatbot. It can only answer a limited set of questions for which it's programmed.

Strong AI

A *strong AI* a superintelligent system that can think, act, ideate, express emotions, and even socially interact like a human being. Such an AI system has consciousness and is aware of its existence.

Strong AI is also called by terms like *Artificial General Intelligence (AGI)* and *Artificial Super Intelligence (ASI)*. This type of AI remains elusive and is only a theoretical concept.

Show me the numbers

When it comes to developments in AI, we are living in an exciting time. There has been an explosion of AI applications in various industries in the past few years. Leading global corporations like Meta, NVIDIA, Microsoft, Google, Amazon, and Apple are investing billions of dollars in AI research, development, and applications.

Let's look at some key statistics related to AI development:

- ◇ The global AI market size was estimated to be $59.67 billion in 2021 and is expected to reach $422.37 billion by 2028 at a CAGR of 39.4%.
- ◇ Between 2015 and 2019, the number of companies utilizing AI services increased by 270%.
- ◇ AI investment is expected to reach $232 billion by 2025.
- ◇ AI is expected to contribute $15.7 trillion to the global GDP by 2030.
- ◇ More than 37% of global organizations use some form of AI in their workplaces.
- ◇ AI is estimated to create 97 million more jobs by 2025.
- ◇ By 2025, 95% of customer interactions in companies would be done by AI applications. Companies would be able to resolve customer queries or even manage marketing communication through AI-powered tools like chatbots, augmented reality, and virtual reality.

Applications of AI in business

Companies, large and small, can reap numerous benefits from AI applications. AI can make business processes more efficient, automate repetitive tasks, personalize customer interactions, improve marketing ROI (revenue per unit of marketing expenditure), and cut costs.

AI can be applied to almost any business domain. These are the sectors that are going to reap the most benefits from AI in the coming years:

◇ **Communication technology:** Voice recognition, translation, customer support, personal assistance, personalization of content, etc.

◇ **Marketing**: Sophisticated marketing analytics, personalized communications, augmented marketing experience, AI-driven customer support, etc.

◇ **Automobile**: Autonomous vehicles, traffic management, route planning, etc.

◇ **Healthcare:** Automated patient data management, more efficient diagnosis, better treatment planning, etc.

◇ **E-commerce**: Virtual shopping environment, voice search, product recommendation, personalized shopping list, etc.

◇ **Retail**: Automated check-out and payment processing, automated replenishment, AI-powered smart stores, etc.

◇ **Banking and financial services:** Better targeting of customers, fraud detection and prevention, automated transactions, etc.

◇ **Energy:** Smart forecasting, resource management, smart meters, failure detection, and prevention, etc.

◇ **Manufacturing**: Automation, robotics, computer vision, 3D printing, etc.

◇ **Logistics and transportation**: Traffic management, route planning, traffic flow analysis, object detection, automated license plate detection, road condition monitoring, etc.

KEY TAKEAWAYS

- Artificial Intelligence (AI) is a branch of computer science focused on creating intelligent machines that can think and function like humans. It has evolved over the past seven decades and encompasses various stages of development, from reactive AI to the theoretical concept of self-aware AI.
- AI systems can be classified as weak or strong, depending on their ability to perform tasks. Currently, most AI applications are weak AI, which are designed for specific tasks, while strong AI remains a theoretical concept that would possess human-like intelligence and consciousness.
- AI has experienced significant growth in recent years, with substantial investments from leading global corporations. Applications of AI span various industries, such as communication technology, healthcare, e-commerce, banking, energy, manufacturing, and logistics, transforming businesses and impacting global GDP.

Chapter 2

MACHINE LEARNING - TEACHING ELEPHANTS TO DANCE THE NEW STEPS

Artificial Intelligence, deep learning, machine learning—whatever you're doing if you don't understand it—learn it. Because otherwise, you're going to be a dinosaur within 3 years.
- Mark Cuban

In June 2014, Eugene Goostman, a 13-year-old Ukrainian boy passed the famous Turing Test at the Royal Society in London. There was nothing remarkable about this event except that Goostman wasn't Ukrainian - nor was he a boy. In fact, it was a chatbot developed by three Russian computer programmers Vladimir Veselov, Eugene Demchenko and Sergey Ulasen.

The Turing Test was developed by Alan Turing in 1950 to determine whether a machine exhibits human intelligence. When a machine, for say, a chatbot or a digital assistant, passes this test, it means the application is displaying human intelligence. Machine Learning (ML) is the fundamental technology behind manifesting human intelligence in smart machines (or smart boys?) like Goostman.

While AI is trying to develop intelligent computer systems, machine learning techniques make these systems truly intelligent.

What is machine learning?

Monday, 16 September 1935 - a column in The Times begins with the following lines:

> *Driven by an electrical motor and controlled by mechanical feeders, this robot rat finds its way through the artificial maze...*

Titled 'Mechanical Rat Finds Way in Maze', the news article describes a 'Robot Rat' navigating a complex maze by learning through trial and error. Robot Rat, one of the earliest demonstrations of machine learning in action, was developed by American psychologist Dr. Stevenson Smith based on the work of another American inventor Thomas Ross. The smart toy shows the core essence of machine learning - enabling machines to apply 'knowledge' and 'experience' to solve a never-seen-before problem.

Machine learning techniques are building computer systems that learn automatically and improve with experience. So, a computer program designed to identify traffic lights can improve on its own with the iterative process of machine learning and better its predictions over time.

The term 'machine learning' was first used in 1959 by the American computer scientist Arthur Samuel, one of the pioneers of AI. In his own words, *machine learning is the field of study that gives computers the ability to learn without being explicitly programmed.*

By definition, machine learning is a specialized branch of AI that trains a machine to execute something in the absence of specific instructions. In simpler words, machine learning helps computer systems emulate the human learning process to improve itself over a period. So machine learning helps improve Facebook's friend suggestions algorithm or make Netflix's suggested watchlist more refined and aligned with your tastes.

Machine learning is intensively used in AI applications like image and speech recognition, recommendation systems on streaming or e-commerce sites, and object detection (for example, traffic lights and pedestrians) in self-driving cars.

Why do we want machines to learn?

Machine learning helps build intelligent machines that can learn from historical data to identify patterns and make efficient decisions without the need for human intervention. It allows a computer to look for patterns in a new data set and automatically build models or programs to predict an outcome. It's applied to situations in which direct programming isn't feasible and we want the machine to make decisions on its own when it encounters new data. Machine learning systems are designed to learn from the data itself rather than relying on any predetermined formula.

So, why do we need machine learning in the first place? Let's explore.

The brief answer is that it's not practical, or outright infeasible in most cases, to train a system with all possible cases that it may encounter in the future. Think about a spam mail filtering system - it cannot be trained with all the possible cases of spam it may need to filter in the future. Machine learning enables a computer to deal with an unknown situation through 'self-learning', such as automatically developing models or programs to analyze new data, for say a new email that looks like spam, and making predictions. This is quite analogous to human learning in which we apply our academic lessons and life experiences to deal with real-life situations which are dynamic and unique.

Machine learning is trying to fulfill the primary goal of AI - building human-like machines. Now the question is how does the elephant learn the new dance steps on its own?

Let's go a bit deeper.

Schooling the machines - how does machine learning work?

Machine learning follows an iterative process to make machines learn and apply their learning like human beings. Let's look at the process of machine learning in its most basic form:

In the first step, a computer system is fed with training data to create an initial machine learning algorithm (a sequence of instructions to solve problems). The type and the quality of data impact the algorithm and its outcome.

In the next step, we feed new input data to the algorithm to check whether the algorithm produces desirable outcomes by comparing the predictions and the results. If the predictions of the algorithm aren't satisfactory, we would retrain the algorithm with more data and repeat the process until the predictions are satisfactory. So, the machine learning algorithm continuously improves on its own and makes optimal predictions.

As you can see, training machine learning algorithms would require millions of individual data points and huge computing power. So, companies with substantial computing power to collect, manage, and process a large volume of data are going to benefit the most from the AI revolution.

To get a better idea of how machine learning works, let's look at the different ways machine learning takes place.

Types of machine learning

There're four broad ways to train machine learning algorithms. Let's have an overview of those.

Supervised machine learning

Supervised machine learning is quite similar to students learning a lesson in the presence of a teacher. In this type of machine learning, an algorithm is trained with a labeled dataset to predict the output. Training with labeled datasets involves tagging some of the inputs with the correct output. The machine can then find a mapping function, like a rule to connect the correct output with the inputs. Next, the machines can extend this learning to apply to new datasets based on the mapping function.

Let's take an example - we can first train a machine-learning algorithm with images of cats and dogs by labeling different parameters like size, shape, colors, eyes, facial features, etc. Now we can expect the algorithm to learn the differentiating rule(s) and segregate new images based on this learning. Supervised machine learning is widely used in fraud detection, image classification, spam filtering, etc.

Unsupervised machine learning

As the name suggests, unsupervised machine learning takes place in the absence of a labeled dataset. In this type of machine learning, the algorithm itself finds a hidden pattern in the unlabelled dataset and makes predictions.

Unsupervised machine learning can literally distinguish the apples from the oranges - if an algorithm is fed a large number of images of apples and oranges, the machine would identify the differentiating factors (like color, shape, texture, etc.) and segregate these images into two categories - apples and oranges. So, if supervised learning is a learning process aided by following rules, unsupervised learning involves learning through experience.

A practical application of unsupervised machine learning is Google News. Google's algorithm can identify different news articles on the same event or topic, like the US presidential election, and organize them under a single category or topic. Unsupervised machine learning is widely used in segmenting customers, detecting anomalies like fraud, and classifying objects.

Semi-supervised learning

This type of machine learning combines both supervised and unsupervised learning. Under semi-supervised learning, an algorithm is trained with both labeled and unlabeled data. Such mixed training helps in overcoming the shortcomings of both modes of learning discussed above.

If we take the analogy of human learning - under supervised learning, a student learns in the presence of an instructor, under unsupervised learning the student relies on self-learning, and lastly under semi-supervised learning the student first learns in the presence of a teacher and then goes back home to revise the concept on his/her own.

Reinforcement learning

Under this process, a system learns and improves performance through continuous feedback. In this type of machine learning, an algorithm predicts outcomes based on trial and error. For each correct prediction, the algorithm gets positive feedback (reward) and for each incorrect prediction, it gets negative feedback (punishment). Over time, the algorithm learns to maximize rewards by correcting and improving its predictions.

The process of machine learning is quite analogous to training your puppy by giving it a treat whenever it shows a desired behavior and punishing it for undesirable actions. Over time, the puppy learns from experience and fine-tunes its behavior with your expectations.

Reinforcement learning is used in various AI applications like robotic automation, image processing, natural language processing, and recommendation system design.

Machine learning applications

Since machine learning is the core component of developing AI, it can be used in almost all business domains. These are some examples of real-life machine-learning applications:

- **Finance and investment:** Credit scoring, trading algorithms (automatic set-ups for trading financial instruments like stocks and currencies), and fraud detection.
- **Computer vision**: Face ID, object and motion detection, robotics, and classification.
- **Pharmaceuticals and healthcare**: Drugs development, detection of tumor and cancer cells, DNA sequencing, and treatment planning.
- **Aerospace**: Anomaly detection, predictive maintenance, space robotics, and unmanned aerial vehicles.
- **Natural language processing**: Voice recognition, parsing, and customer support.
- **Manufacturing**: Automation and robotics, quality control, automated logistics, product design, and product development.
- **E-commerce:** Product recommendation, virtual assistance, customer support, and enhanced shopping experience.

Machine learning trends to watch out for

Machine learning is an evolving and highly dynamic field. These are some of the new trends in machine learning which can disrupt many industries soon:

Foundation models

These are AI applications trained with an immense amount of data, which can not only discover patterns but also accumulate knowledge. For example, ChatGPT can create content and answer search queries, which can disrupt traditional search engines like Google. While a

Google Search leads to a list of relevant web links, ChatGPT provides more specific and direct answers to our search queries. Moreover, we can ask ChatGPT follow-up questions and have a human-like conversation. Which leads to the question - are the days of Google Search numbered?

Embedded machine learning

It's a branch of machine learning that allows machine learning applications to work on various devices. Combined with the Internet of Things (IoT), a network of connected objects, embedded machine learning helps in building smart homes, smart offices, and various devices of specialized utilities.

No-code machine learning

This technique helps people with little or no coding knowledge to build machine learning algorithms to suit their specific needs. No-code machine learning can lead to faster and wider adoption of machine learning.

Creative machine learning

Various creative machine learning models like Midjourney, DALL-E, and Stable Diffusion help in extending human creativity and imagination. Users can create images, artwork, designs, etc. using these tools.

Multimodal machine learning

This type of machine learning enables a machine to process inputs simultaneously received through multiple modes like texts, images, videos, etc. Multimodal machine learning aims at building machines with more enhanced and human-like information processing capabilities to interact with the environment more efficiently. GPT-4, the next iteration of OpenAI's GPT model is confirmed to have multimodal capability.

KEY TAKEAWAYS

- ◇ Machine learning is a branch of AI that enables computers to learn from data and improve their performance over time without explicit programming. It is used in various applications, such as image recognition, recommendation systems, and self-driving cars.
- ◇ There are four main types of machine learning: supervised, unsupervised, semi-supervised, and reinforcement learning. Each type has its unique approach to training algorithms, with supervised learning relying on labeled datasets, and unsupervised learning focusing on identifying patterns in unlabeled data.
- ◇ Machine learning is an evolving field with emerging trends like foundation models, embedded machine learning, no-code machine learning, creative machine learning, and multimodal machine learning. These trends have the potential to disrupt industries and create new opportunities for AI applications in various domains.

Chapter 3

GENERATIVE AI - WHEN MACHINES TELL STORIES

Artificial intelligence is one of the most profound things we're working on as humanity. It is more profound than fire or electricity
*- **Sundar Pichai, CEO of Google***

In the 1860s, Charles Lutwidge Dodgson, popularly known by his pen name Lewis Carroll, spent about 2 years writing his celebrated work Alice's Adventures in Wonderland. Those were different days. In December 2022, Ammaar Reshi, a Silicon Valley techie coauthored a children's book and got it published in little more than 2 days. Titled 'Alice and Sparkle', the 26-page long fiction depicts the story of a young girl Alice embarking on an adventurous journey with her own robot Sparkle to make the world a better place. Although not as illustrious as Carroll's masterpiece, what makes Reshi's book truly unique is it was actually written by OpenAI's advanced chatbot named ChatGPT and illustrated by another AI tool Midjourney.

Times have changed and we have now built machines that can tell stories, compose lyrics, prepare recipes, draw realistic images, write codes, discover drugs, and design microchips - activities that were earlier unimaginable without human creativity. The enabling technology behind these content-creating AI applications is called generative AI.

These days generative AI is a trending topic mainly for the fun, and often bizarre, elements like Dall-E (OpenAI's tool generating images from text prompts) creating images of an astronaut in space riding a horse or a Raphael-style portrait of Madonna and Child eating pizza, or even ChatGPT instructing how to remove a peanut butter sandwich from a VCR in the style of a biblical verse.

Figure 3: *My Dall-E generated image of Warren Buffett and Prince Harry working out at a gym together (source: Midjourney)*

But beyond this noise, some real actions are going on in this space. Let's look at these headlines:

- ◇ DeepMind's protein-folding AI cracks biology's biggest problem.
- ◇ Lancôme creates ground-breaking AI beauty devices to help people

with disabilities apply makeup.

- AI tools such as ChatGPT to drive the digital transformation of insurance.
- Shutterstock Introduces Generative AI to its All-In-One Creative Platform.
- Is Google Displacing Musicians with Its New Generative AI System: MusicLM?
- Generating 3D Models from text with Nvidia's MAGIC3D.
- The Generative AI Revolution is Creating the Next Phase of Autonomous Enterprise.

Generative AI is powerful and it can literally revolutionize almost every business domain. According to a January 2023 report by technology research firm Gartner, venture capital firms have invested over $1.7 billion in this technology in the previous 3 years. A lion's share of this funding was made for AI-enabled drug discovery and AI software coding.

The same report predicts generative AI to create 30% of all marketing messages from large companies by 2025, up from just 2% in 2022. More interestingly, Gartner expects we would have at least one major blockbuster film by 2030 in which almost 90% of the film would be created by generative AI.

So what's this fuss all about? Let's find out.

First things first – what's generative AI?

We asked the same question to ChatGPT, one of the most sophisticated generative AI tools developed so far, and here is its reply:

This nifty form of machine learning allows computers to generate all sorts of new and exciting content, from music and art to entire virtual worlds. And it's not just for fun—generative AI has plenty of practical uses too, like creating new product designs and optimizing business processes. So why wait?

ChatGPT gives us a correct answer - both technically and grammatically. And look at the use of words and the tone – who can say this hasn't been answered by a computer science professor in a pleasant mood?

In a playful banter, we followed this up with ChatGPT and asked it to answer the same question - but, this time as a poem. Here came the reply at its creative best:

Generative AI, a muse so bright,
Creating new things with computational might.
A system trained, with rules in hand,
To generate output, at its command.
From data learned, it weaves a tale,
Of images, text, and audio, so rare and stale.
Not just a copy, but something unique,
A novel creation, its artistic mystique.
So let it dream, and let it play,
And watch as it generates, a work of art each day.

Generative AI is pretty much what the poem indicates - AI applications that can automatically create new data like texts, images, codes, simulations, animation, videos, and even recipes for banana-flavored chocolate chip cookies in a matter of seconds. It's powered by machine learning techniques that train algorithms to generate original content on command. The content created by generative AI would be synthetic and completely new. Can you imagine the endless possibilities generative AI could create given that AI teams spend nearly 50-80% of their time collecting, cleaning, and labeling data?

Using generative AI, we can generate new text (say, a marketing email), create new images, translate images (like changing an MRI image to a CT scan image), enhance images (for example, improving a blurred image to a clear one), generate speech from text, create new audio/video, build 3D models, generate synthetic data (for example, different driving conditions to train an autonomous vehicle) and even write code to build new algorithms.

Generative AI vs. Discriminative AI

Until very recently, most AI applications were based on discriminative models. As we previously discussed, a discriminative AI model is good at separating apples from oranges – quite literally. These AI models are trained to observe and classify patterns in the training data. So, fed with a large number of images of apples and oranges, these models eventually learn the differences and when we feed new data (say, an image of a new apple) to the trained system, it can successfully classify it and place it in the right category.

Generative AI is quite different – it's a breakthrough in AI advancement because it can generate a completely new image (or texts, audio, video, and much more) of an apple or orange (or anything else) automatically. It learns the patterns and building blocks and then creates something unique on its own. So, next time you need to generate a unique image of a juicy Fuji apple for your food blog, you know where to get it. In simple words, generative AI empowers machines to be creative and build unique stuff from scratch.

Generative AI opens a whole new world of opportunities and applications. While you can ask it to create an image of a baby panda walking around Time Square with a Starbucks coffee in one hand to amuse your child, a scientist can use generative AI to develop an anti-body structure that can neutralize a new virus, say, a more potent variant of the COVID-19.

What makes all these feasible? Let's dig deeper, because it has significant implications for those of us interested in investing in the AI revolution.

How does generative AI work?

In its most basic form, generative AI is the result of the holy trinity of data, models, and immense computing power. Models show how certain inputs can be transformed into outputs and how an immense amount of data (OpenAI's GPT3, the previous avatar of ChatGPT, was trained with 45 terabytes of text data – that's little less than 200 miles of bookshelf space) can be used to train the models. The training eventually leads to algorithms like Google's LaMDA (a conversational AI model) or Stability AI's Stable Diffusion (a text-to-image model) that can generate new data.

Let's use an analogy to understand it better – Dall-E is a young painter with vibrant energy who can demonstrate his creativity through colors. You show him millions of paintings of different artists with descriptions of as many elements as you like – style, color, landscapes, shapes, and sizes. Eventually, Dall-E would learn to combine all these elements and develop a fresh and original painting on your command – pretty simple! No, it's not.

Generative AI tools are the results of complex mathematical techniques, gigantic computing power, hundreds of millions worth of funding, and thousands of hours of effort by top computer scientists. So realistically, in the short term, only large companies like Google, Microsoft, Meta, and NVIDIA, which have the best talent, piles of cash, and cutting-edge technology, have been able to build such models.

Types of generative AI models

There are different approaches to building generative AI models based on what we want the models to create. Let's look at the three primary approaches to developing generative AI models:

Generative Adversarial Networks (GANs)

GANs use two competing neural networks (algorithms that mimic learning in the human brain) to generate synthetic data that's indistinguishable from real data. GANs were introduced in 2014 by Ian Goodfellow and other researchers at the University of Montreal.

The two neural networks in GANs are called *Generator* and *Discriminator*. The *Generator* creates plausible or fake data to test the *Discriminator* while the *Discriminator* is tasked with identifying the fake data. The Discriminator receives data from two sources - one from the real data (they serve as a positive sample) fed into the model and the other from the fake data (they serve as a negative sample) created by the generator. The ultimate objective is to create synthetic data that passes for real data.

Let's simplify this. Suppose you have a database of real 100-dollar bills. Now you make the Generator create fake 100-dollar bills and then program the Discriminator to identify the fake bills.

GANs are widely used in generating images, voices, and videos.

Transformer models

First described in 2017, these models are among the newest inventions in the machine learning space. In simple words, a transformer model is a neural network that can study context by looking at relationships in sequential data, for example, words in a sentence. The meaning of a sentence changes drastically by changing the sequence of words. Transformer models can detect these changes in meaning, which makes them excellent candidates for creating tools like ChatGPT that can carry out intelligent conversations, write essays and translate from one language to another.

Transformer models are primarily used in natural language processing. For example, Google uses it in translation or auto-completion of search queries.

Variational AutoEncoders (VAEs)

An *AutoEncoder* is a neural network that undergoes unsupervised learning to create a new dataset. An *AutoEncoder* is first trained with input data. The network then picks up salient features of the input data and tries to reconstruct data based on this learning. Finally, the network creates an approximation of the input as an output.

An *AutoEncoder* has two components – an *encoder* and a *decoder*. The *encoder* picks up the most important features from the training input data and the *decoder* then tries to reconstruct the original data from the encoded features. A *Variational AutoEncoder* is slightly modified from a standard *AutoEncoder* – instead of encoding an input as a single point, it encodes in a probabilities manner to create the original output more efficiently. Variational *AutoEncoders* are extensively used in regenerating images.

Use cases of generative AI

For decades, scientists have been baffled by the question of how amino acids twist and fold in different ways to give the eventual 3D shape of proteins, the building blocks of our bodies. AlphaFold, a generative AI model of DeepMind (a subsidiary of Google), has just achieved this gargantuan feat of determining the 3D shape of protein - solving one of biology's biggest riddles and opening a floodgate of opportunities in biological research and drug discovery.

This is just one of the numerous practical applications of generative AI that create huge business opportunities for firms willing to exploit these technologies. According to Brian Burke, Research VP for Technology Innovation at Gartner, *early foundation models like ChatGPT focus on the ability of generative AI to augment creative work, but by 2025, we expect more than 30% — up from zero today — of new drugs and materials to be systematically discovered using generative AI techniques.*

It will be an understatement to say that generative AI would disrupt almost all industries sooner than expected. According to a report by Acumen Research and Consulting, the global generative AI market would be worth $110 billion in 2030 up from $7.9 billion in 2021 - a CAGR of a whopping 34.3%. Generative AI has already generated more than $100 million in revenue in three product categories - coding, copywriting, and image creation. There's an increased interest among consumers and businesses regarding developments in this space.

Going by the projections and research by Gartner, these are the business domains that would benefit the most from generative AI advancements:

- **Drug design:** Generative AI can drastically cut the cost of drug discovery and the time required to bring new drugs to market from 3-6 years to a few months.
- **Chip manufacturing:** Generating AI can significantly lower the chip manufacturing lifecycle by optimizing component placement.
- **Material science:** Generative AI can immensely benefit industries like automobiles, aerospace, medical equipment, and electronics through the development of new materials with specific properties.
- **Synthetic data:** The growth of the digital economy heavily depends on data, which is increasingly becoming a scarce resource because of privacy concerns. Generative AI can develop synthetic data (say, patient data that mimics original data) which can benefit industries ranging from retail to healthcare.
- **Design of parts:** Generative AI can revolutionize design by developing products that meet specific requirements to revolutionize industries like manufacturing, electronics, aerospace, and medical devices.

KEY TAKEAWAYS

- Generative AI is a rapidly evolving technology that enables machines to create new and original content, such as text, images, audio, video, and more. It has the potential to revolutionize various industries, from drug design to chip manufacturing.
- Generative AI models are created using various methods, each suited for different purposes. Some of the main techniques include GANs, which involve two competing algorithms to create realistic data; Transformer models, which excel at understanding and generating text by analyzing word relationships; and VAEs, which focus on recreating and improving input data. These approaches have diverse applications, such as language understanding and image creation.
- The global generative AI market is expected to grow significantly, with a projected worth of $110 billion by 2030. Industries that stand to benefit the most include drug design, chip manufacturing, material science and part design, as generative AI can drastically cut costs, reduce development time, and create novel solutions.

Chapter 4

INVESTING IN MEGATRENDS - THE ART OF NOT MISSING THE WOOD FOR THE TREES

The trend is your friend until the end when it bends
- Ed Seykota

On October 11, 2011, meteorologists observed a tropical disturbance crossing the southern part of Central America, which entered the Eastern Pacific the next day. There was no major anomaly reported in the following few days. The development was given a nothing-much-to-worry-about status of a 'tropical depression' on October 20. In the next 24 hours, a rare confluence of climatic factors - a higher-than-usual ocean surface temperature, lower speed of the atmospheric wind, and a higher-than-average relative humidity - took the disturbance to a far more serious level of a Category 5 storm. The following day, Hurricane Patricia became the most intense tropical cyclone ever recorded in the Western Hemisphere, with the maximum sustained winds speed reaching 215 mph.

Hurricane Patricia, the strongest storm by windspeed ever recorded, was one of the most extreme climatic events observed on earth. It was unique in many aspects - the sudden convergence of several environmental factors, the complete failure of weather models to predict its development, and the never-seen-before rapidity of a storm's progress. Weather forecasting is complex and far from perfect. But events like Hurricane Patricia show how seemingly gradual and small-scale changes can snowball into something gigantic, irreversible, and extremely consequential.

The world of investing is dynamic and in a constant state of flux. Over time, many investment themes and trends - both short and long-term - emerge with the promise of above-average market returns. Some trends build up pretty fast and in a very unpredictable way - very similar to Hurricane Patricia.

Most of these windows of opportunity close long before the average investor can cash in on the trend. Then there are trends which build up over a long period but eventually become extremely large-scale, global, and permanent. These trends change the business world or even the entire economy and society for decades to come.

These are megatrends.

Making sense of megatrends

The Oxford English Dictionary defines a megatrend as *an important shift in the progress of a society or of any other particular field or activity.* Megatrends are often gradual (though rapid in some cases) economic, social, or technological changes that eventually become massive, all-pervasive, irreversible, and global. They become the mainstream after disrupting the existing systems, business conditions, the overall economy, or even the entire human society. In short - megatrends are sustainable and transformative changes that shape our collective future.

Can you think of some recent megatrends?

Let's look at the Internet. Are we ever going back to those days when getting even basic information like the telephone number of a local plumber was quite a hassle? Who would like to drive to a travel agency's office again to book an air ticket? In 2022, there were about 5.3 billion Internet users (around 70% of the world population) up from a meager 361 million (6% of the world population) in 2000. The Internet is massive, global, and irreversible - it's a megatrend and the world will never be the same as before (at least in our most distant imagination) and because of its implications in almost all spheres of our society.

If we look at the rapidly changing economic, social, and technological landscape, we would be able to see some megatrends which are already underway - global warming and climate change, breakthroughs in renewable energy, rapid urbanization, demographic shifts across countries, human longevity, technological breakthroughs, and shifts in global economic power.

When capitalized on, these megatrends can give great investment outcomes. Had you invested $1,000 in Amazon, one of the largest beneficiaries of the Internet megatrend, in 2002, the investment would be worth $218,793.08 in 2022 - an average annual growth of 30.9% in these 20 years. Compare this to the not-so-lucrative 6.29% average annual return by the S&P 500 in the same period. Irrespective of the hiccups during the dot.com bubble going bust, the leading Internet companies of today have created immense value for the stockholders in the last two and half decades.

Despite the many opportunities, megatrends often produce extreme challenges and risks to mitigate. Think of the rising instances of cyber fraud and digital crimes that take place using the Internet. According to an estimate by Cybersecurity Ventures, a leading global researcher on cybercrime, globally cybercrime will cost $10.5 trillion a year by 2025, up from $3 trillion in 2015. However, where there's a crisis, there's an opportunity. We can already see rapid progress in the cybersecurity industry, which is poised to grow at a CAGR of 13.4% annually with public companies like Palo Alto Networks (941% return since 2012 IPO), Fortinet (561% return since 2018 IPO) and Zscaler (181% return since 2019 IPO) delighting shareholders along the way.

Lastly, a megatrend doesn't exist in isolation. More often than not, one megatrend overlaps or influences another in an increasingly interconnected world. The overlapping and interconnectedness of megatrends create many investment themes with high potential returns. The confluence of advanced computing, smartphones, and the Internet has made e-commerce possible, which is a $16.6 trillion industry as of 2022. E-commerce companies like eBay (12,915% return since 1998 IPO), MercadoLibre (4,116% return since 2007 IPO) and Shopify (271% returns since 2018 IPO) have created substantial wealth for investors over the years.

3 major recent megatrends - learning from the history

Spanish-born American philosopher George Santayana once famously said, *we must welcome the future, remembering that soon it will be the past; and we must respect the past, remembering that it was once all that was humanly possible.* The past can be an extremely crucial guide in our investing journey. Even though not completely in the past as these developments are still evolving and unfolding, we can draw valuable investment lessons from these recent two megatrends:

Mobile technology

In 1926, legendary American inventor Nikola Tesla envisioned an amazingly simple

communication device that a person *will be able to carry one in his vest pocket.* It took another six decades for the first mobile device to be commercially launched - Motorola DynaTAC 8000X in 1983. We had to wait more than 10 years before a smartphone was introduced - IBM Simon in 1994.

With a slow initial adoption rate, similar to most other emerging technologies, it took about 17 years for total smartphone users to grow from a paltry user base of 30,000 in 1994 to an astounding 1 billion figure by 2011. The real inflection point came around this time - the number of mobile phone users reached 5.44 billion in little more than a decade by the end of 2022 with 4 out of 5 of these devices being a smartphone. The total number of smartphone users is estimated to reach 7.5 billion by 2026.

Mobile technology is a megatrend as it has revolutionized communication and disrupted the business world along with impacting societies at a massive scale. By the end of 2022, more than 60% of Internet users accessed the web using mobile devices. Over 70% of time spent on consuming digital content like music, videos, games, audiobooks and news happens through mobiles. In 2022, the size of global smartphone shipments was 1.2 billion earning more than $409 billion in revenue - 48% of which went to the market leader Apple.

With a myriad of applications - ranging from listening to music, accessing emails, playing games, or buying goods and services - smartphones have become an indispensable part of modern society. The megatrend also presented investors with a huge window of opportunity for above-average returns. Had you invested $1,000 in Apple stock in 2007, the year in which its charismatic founder Steve Jobs launched the first iPhone, your investment would have been worth a whopping $46,333 by 2022 - that's an astounding 46X return in 15 years!

E-commerce

Can you even imagine today's global economy without e-commerce - with online businesses selling more than 20% of all goods and services online? The ball started rolling when the first legitimate e-commerce transaction, a CD of Sting's *Ten Summoner's Tales* sold for $12.48 plus shipping costs, took place in 1994. The very next year e-commerce pioneers Amazon and eBay started operations.

Wide adoption of the Internet and rapid advancement in mobile technologies led to the rapid growth of e-commerce in the last 2 decades. Global e-commerce sales are expected to reach $7.4 trillion by 2025 from $4.9 trillion in 2021 with a double-digit annual growth rate. It took Amazon 5 years to reach the first $1 billion in sales. With its annual revenue of $513.98 billion in 2022, Amazon now earns $1 billion in less than a day!

E-commerce has transformed businesses, economies, and societies. The developing markets have been immensely benefitting from e-commerce with most of the fastest growing e-commerce markets belonging to these countries. The Latin American market (including Peru, Brazil, Argentina, Chile, Colombia, and Mexico) clocked online sales of $104 billion in 2022 - a 22.4% rise from $85 billion in 2021. India, one of the top-5 fastest growing e-commerce markets, experienced 25.5% sales growth in 2022. China with online sales of $2.8 trillion, continued to be the top e-commerce market in the same year.

Today, e-marketplaces are the preferred shopping destinations of young people as more than 33% of e-commerce customers belong to the 18-34 age group. With every $0.20 of $1 spent on goods and services going to e-commerce companies, e-commerce has created massive entrepreneurial opportunities. 2022 saw 3.78 billion people shopping online - a number expected to continue growing over the coming years and creating more value for investors, consumers, and businesses.

Electric Vehicles (EVs)

The EV megatrend is comparatively new and at a nascent stage compared to smartphones and e-commerce. The main driving forces behind this megatrend are increasing concerns about global warming, a looming energy crisis, and the reduced cost of lithium-ion batteries. The current EV revolution is the beginning of a long-term shift in the automobile industry. Global EV sales nearly doubled between 2020 and 2021 to reach 6.6 million vehicles. In 2022, total EV sales stood at 7.8 million units - about 10% of the total auto sales for the year. This shows a sharp rise in EV sales in the last few years given that EVs constituted only 1% of all automobiles sold in 2015. Morgan Stanley expects EVs to contribute 90% of all auto sales by 2050.

An EV operates on 100% electric power thereby drastically reducing our dependence on fossil fuels and lowering emission levels. The International Energy Agency (IEA) expects 145 million EVs on the road by 2030. This would be a major achievement toward meeting the net-zero emission goal by 2050. According to an estimate by Bloomberg, EVs can lower global oil demand by as much as 2 million barrels per day by 2023.

Battery cost constitutes around one-third of the total cost of an EV. As batteries become cheaper to produce, the demand for EVs is expected to skyrocket in the coming years. There're also several favorable factors driving the growth of the industry - automakers committing billions of dollars, improvement in EV performance, reduction in costs, and favorable government policies. The total revenue of the global EV market is expected to reach $457.60 billion and $858 billion by 2023 and 2027 respectively. The huge market potential of EVs has created a tremendous opportunity for investors - especially in the market leaders BYD Auto and Tesla which control over 33% of the market.

Why AI is a megatrend to watch out for

Permacrisis, defined by the Collins English Dictionary as *an extended period of instability and insecurity, esp one resulting from a series of catastrophic events,* was the word of the year in 2022. It's an apt description of our recent times plagued by a once-in-100-years pandemic, economic roller coaster ride, intense geo-political tension, a hanging threat of nuclear war, and multi-decade-high inflation topped with a lurking recession.

But, there's a brighter side to it.

If history is our guide, a time of crisis is often followed by a long period of innovation, growth, and prosperity. Post-World War - II economic expansion, a more resilient financial system after the global financial crisis, and rapid innovation in renewable energy faced with a global energy crisis - stand testimony to this phenomenon. A rapid expansion of the digital economy during the pandemic has catalyzed rapid growth in AI and related technologies. The stats are astounding.

The global AI market is estimated to reach $1.6 trillion by 2030 with a CAGR of 38.1% from 2022 to 2030. North America is expected to account for the largest share of this market. AI appears as a recurring investment theme and a megatrend in research reports of almost all major consulting firms including PwC, BlackRock, and Deloitte.

The Gartner Hype Cycle for Emerging Technologies 2022 includes Accelerated AI automation as one of the 3 key emerging technology trends. The other two are evolving/expanding immersive experiences and optimized technologist delivery. The Hype Cycle shows the stages of evolution of different emerging technologies. Investcorp's – IMD global survey results released in January 2023 predicts Digitization & AI to be the number 1 dominating megatrend for the next 30 years according to investors in all the regions surveyed - US, Europe, and the Middle East. The survey also revealed 8 out of 10 global institutional investors are betting big on the AI space.

With the convergence of several crucial factors - ranging from huge institutional investment, rapid technological breakthrough, and competitive innovation - a new Hurricane Patricia is building up fast and furious. This time it's in the AI space.

KEY TAKEAWAYS

- Megatrends are massive, global, and irreversible changes that shape our collective future. They can offer substantial investment opportunities and have the potential to transform economies and societies. Some recent examples include mobile technology, e-commerce, and electric vehicles.
- Artificial Intelligence (AI) is emerging as a significant megatrend, with the potential to disrupt various industries and drive innovation. The global AI market is estimated to reach $1.6 trillion by 2030, with numerous factors supporting its rapid growth.
- Identifying and capitalizing on megatrends can yield above-average returns for investors. However, it's essential to understand the potential risks and challenges associated with these trends and consider the interconnectedness of different megatrends when making investment decisions.

Chapter 5

ISAAC NEWTON, TULIPS, AND MARIJUANA - LEARNINGS FROM HYPE, BOOMS, AND BUSTS

The four most dangerous words in investing are
'this time it's different'
*- **John Templeton.***

I can calculate the movement of stars but not the madness of men. These were the famous words of Sir Isaac Newton, arguably the greatest physicist and mathematician ever, after losing a fortune in a stock market investment. There's an interesting story behind it.

It was in the 1710s when Newton was one of the early investors in the South Sea Company - a firm primarily set up to manage British Government debt. After initial years of stable returns, the stock started skyrocketing in 1720 when the government allowed the company to take over its debt. Increased public interest soon turned into a frenzy. Well aware of how things can end up badly, Newton exited the market in early 1720 with a handsome profit of £20, 000. South Sea's stock price continued climbing up through the summer. From £128 in January, the price kept moving up to £330 in March and £550 in May. Everyone wanted to have those stocks which apparently could only go up in the future. Who would like to miss the opportunity when neighbors were getting richer every day?

It would be an understatement to say Newton was a genius - he invented calculus that changed the world and his laws of motion are the foundation of classical mechanics. Yet he fell for the FOMO trap - fear of missing out on an opportunity that everyone else was cashing on. The great Sir Isaac Newton bought South Sea Company stocks again at around the peak with all his previous profits and some more. The stock continued climbing up before finally reaching £1,000 by early August. It was too good to be true. What next?

The rest is history - the stock price started crashing with initial profit-taking by early investors and then a large number of investors rushed for the exit at whatever price available. Panicked, Newton decided to sell and exit the market when the price crashed 70-80% from its peak. Before the end of the year, the stock bottomed out at around the initial price of £100.

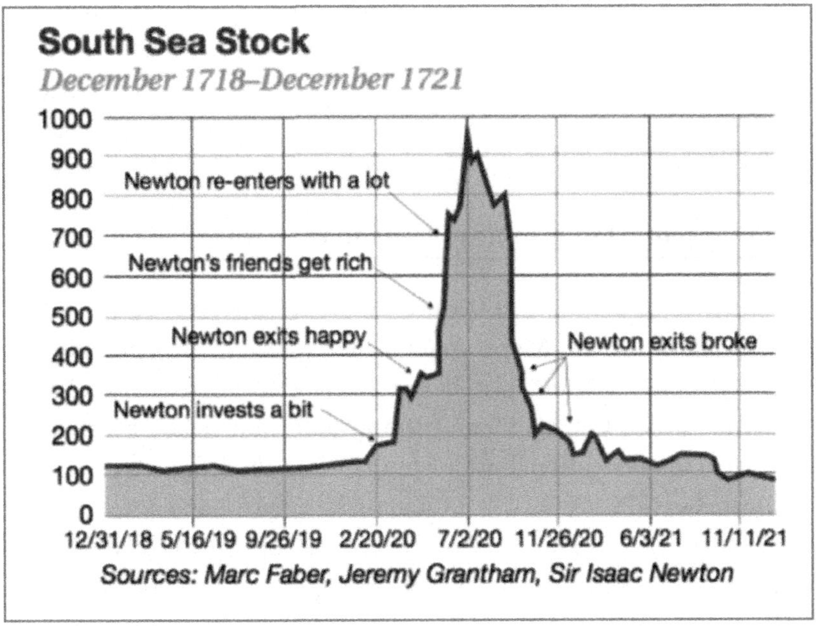

Figure 4: *Isaac Newton's investments in the South Sea Company – note the dates, these refer to the 18th Century, not the 21st (Source: Marc Faber)*

The investment had a major blow to Newton's net worth. According to estimates, the extent of his loss would be around £3.68 million at today's price. Legends say Newton forbade anyone to mention the name of the South Sea in his presence for the rest of his life.

The history of investing is full of examples of asset prices going rapidly high driven by irrational behavior, hype, and mass hysteria every one or two decades. These events follow the same old template - the arrival of a new investment theme, smart money entering the market to fuel initial price rise, euphoria and mass participation, hysterical price rise, profit taking, and then panic to exit. They end up making a few smart investors super-rich while wreaking havoc on the financial health of millions.

These events are market bubbles.

AI is hot and happening - it's an emerging technology with massive commercial potential. Plus, there's a rapidly increasing interest from companies, investors, media, and even the government. In short, conditions are perfect for the next big bubble to form in the AI space.

Exploring market bubbles - how do they form?

In April 2019, a headline on the prestigious Wall Street Journal reads: *Legalization in Canada Sparks Rally in Marijuana Stocks - Big beverage makers also jump into the fray, hoping to capitalize on the growth.* About 6 months earlier, Canada became the second country (after Uruguay) to legalize the recreational use of cannabis. In the US, medical use of marijuana was already legal in 33 states while recreational use was legal in 10 states. The dominant view was recreational cannabis is going to be the next big thing with Canada alone projected to contribute $8 billion in revenue by 2020 and the US market contributing another $23.4 billion in revenue by 2022.

What followed next was a frenzy for rushing into the cannabis business with large companies like Constellation Brands, AB InBev, and Molson Coors contributing billions of dollars of investment, new firms going public, and retail investors adventuring for a fun ride.

Tilray, a major global producer of medical and recreational cannabis, launched its IPO at $17 in July 2018. The stock climbed to as high as $300 on 19th September, taking its market cap to a whopping $157 billion. The numbers were quite astounding for a firm that reported revenue of $17 million and a bigger loss of $18 million in the previous 6 months. The previous day, the company got a regulator's nod to import medical marijuana for testing. By the end of the next year, the stock was trading at around $16 - lower than its IPO price. Today the stock trades at a market cap of just $2.53 a share after a reverse stock split, down more than 90% from IPO.

Another leading giant Canopy Growth saw its stocks tumbling up to 60% between April and December 2019. The aggregate market value of all marijuana stocks was down by more than 50% by the end of 2019. All those high growth projections and earning multiples vanished in thin air when reality set in - the industry was exposed to multiple challenges of oversupply, competition from the black market, and lower-than-expected demand.

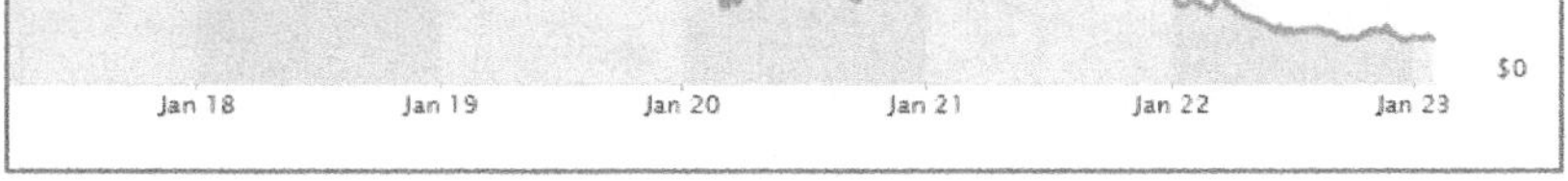

Figure 5: *Price performance of the Horizons Marijuana Life Sciences Index ETF since inception, (Source: MarketWatch)*

The marijuana industry is a perfect example of what market bubbles are and how they are formed.

In simple words, a market bubble is a rapid increase in the price of an asset (like stocks, bonds, real estate, gold, and oil) in a short period followed by a rapid decline. Such an astounding and fast asset price appreciation is mainly fueled by massive speculative demand for a new industry (legal marijuana), company (South Sea), or technology (the Internet) with little consideration for fundamentals (real profitability, market competition, challenges, and company financials). The high price eventually becomes unsustainable as the industry fails to deliver on the promises of spectacular growth and profitability. Disillusionment sets in and the asset price crashes to its fundamental value or even much lower.

There're generally four stages of a market bubble - the stealth phase when smart money enters, the awareness phase at which big institutional investors start putting money in, mania phase in which a large crowd of retail investors jumps in swayed by intense media coverage and enthusiasm and lastly the blow-off phase when the bubble bursts and expectations meet reality.

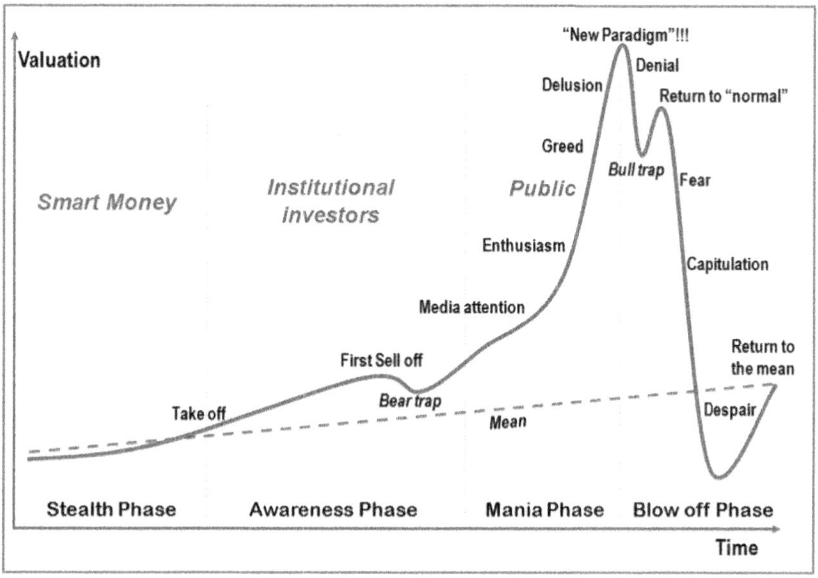

Figure 6: *The 4 stages of a market bubble (Source: Wikimedia Commons)*

3 of the biggest market bubbles in history

Financial bubbles are not new phenomena and they have been taking place for centuries. It may happen in a new industry, a new company, or a new technology. But the rapid boom and bust in asset prices driven by greed, enthusiasm, and herd mentality are historical and universal.

Let's look at 3 of the most noteworthy market bubbles that ever happened.

Tulip mania

Who would like to pay $1 million for a tulip bulb, no matter how rare it is? Well, it may make sense for someone who is hoping to sell it to someone else for $1.5 million! This is exactly what happened in Holland during the Dutch golden age when the price of tulip bulbs reached astronomical prices. At the peak of the bubble in 1636-37, the price of a piece of rare tulip bulb equaled six times the average wage level.

The tulip was an exotic flower introduced to Dutch society from the Middle East through the Spice route. Soon the imported flower caught the fascination of Holland's affluent class. The merchant middle class followed their richer neighbors and started demanding tulips as a status symbol. According to the Library of Economics and Liberty, *the rage among the Dutch to possess [tulip bulbs] was so great that the ordinary industry of the country was neglected, and the population, even to its lowest dregs, embarked on the tulip trade.* However, the supply couldn't keep pace with the soaring demand.

In the 1630s, the price of tulip bulbs was rising in leaps and bounds. At its peak in 1636-37, the rarest bulbs were selling above $1 million at today's price while an average bulb was selling at around $50,000 - $150,000. At one point in 1637, prices rose 1,100% in a month. Huge profit potential attracted many suppliers while people from other professions joined the tulip trade.

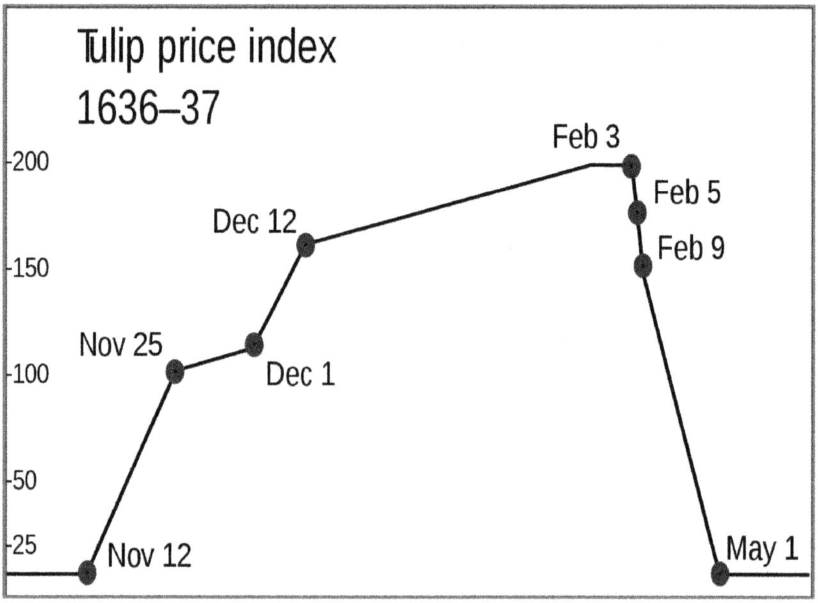

***Figure** 7: The fast expanding tulip bubble (Source: Wikimedia Commons)*

In 1637, the high price was no longer sustainable. Many buyers purchased on credit hoping to recover after selling at an even higher price. As the price started falling, holders of bulbs were forced to sell at any price available. Ultimately the price of tulips crashed leading to economic disasters for most traders. There were many suppliers and no buyers of the coveted tulips, the value of which fell to near zero.

Dot-com bubble

Also called the Internet bubble, the dot-com bubble took place between 1995-2001 during which Internet-related companies experienced rapid stock appreciation followed by a gigantic crash. The Internet, introduced in the 1990s, was a real technological breakthrough after many decades. It came with the promise of revolutionizing businesses and the larger society. The boundless commercial potential of the Internet attracted massive interest from venture capitalists, traditional investors, and technology companies. What followed was a rush to build one of those 'dot-com' companies to change the world or to invest in one to get rich sooner.

Figure 8: *The Rise of and Fall of the NASDAQ 100 (1994-2004) (Source: Investopedia)*

The sudden influx of money fueled by institutional investment, retail participation, and media hype led to a rapid appreciation of Internet stocks. In little more than 4 years (1996-2000), tech-heavy NASDAQ went up from the 1,000 level to cross 5,000. In the extreme phase of the bubble formation, NASDAQ appreciated more than 70% in just 6 months - from 2,978 in October 1999 to an intraday high of 5,132 in March 2000. The craze was so intense that companies could outperform their peers by as much as 63% simply by adding .com, .net, or Internet to their names. Simply, no one was looking at the fundamentals in the fear of missing out. In 1999, Qualcomm's stock appreciated by 2,619% while 19 other large-cap stocks rose by more than 900%.

The Internet bubble finally burst when NASDAQ fell more than 75% between March 2000 and October 2022, wiping out more than $5 trillion worth of valuation from the market. In 2000, out of 280 stocks in the Bloomberg Internet Index, 79 stocks were down more than 90% from their 52-week high (including Amazon), while a further 72 stocks were down between 80-89%. The bursting of the dot-com bubble led to an 8-month-long recession in the USA in 2001. Only 48% of all dot-com companies survived through 2004, albeit at a much lower valuation.

US housing market bubble

The US housing market bubble took place in the 2000s. The bubble is also known as the subprime mortgage crisis as increased lending to subprime customers (borrowers with lower creditworthiness) led to the crisis. One of the driving forces behind the increased lending was the US government's policy to make affordable housing more accessible to people with lower incomes and savings. Since the borrowers belonged to a high-risk category, the interest rate was higher.

By 2002, Government-sponsored mortgage lenders Fannie Mae and Freddie Mac extended mortgage credit worth more than $3 trillion. To make things worse, US consumer debt soared to an all-time high level of $2 trillion by 2004. Everything was going fine for the borrowers and lenders as long as housing prices kept soaring between 1997-2006. During this period, the price of a typical American house increased by up to 124%. However, a time bomb was ticking. Robert R. Prechter Jr., the founder of Elliott Wave International, warned in his 2002 book Conquer the Crash: *confidence is the only thing holding up this giant house of cards.*

The housing price in the USA peaked in 2006 and subsequently started declining later in 2006 and 2007. US home values fell by 26% between June 2006 and November 2009. Borrowers were faced with falling value of their homes coupled with higher mortgage payments adjusted due to the Adjustable Rate these borrowers signed up for but could not afford. Homeowners started defaulting on their mortgage payments at a massive scale and the foreclosure rate soared in 2006-07. The chain reaction set by the housing bubble burst ultimately led to a much bigger crisis - the 2008 Global Financial Crisis, which was the largest financial crisis in the world after the Great Depression in the 1930s.

Avoiding the FOMO trap while investing in AI

The Oracle of Omaha Warren Buffet famously said - *it's good to learn from your mistakes. It's better to learn from other people's mistakes.* While investing in a megatrend, it's easy for an investor to get swayed by emotion and jump on the bandwagon. However, if history is to be our guide, we must walk the tightrope balancing rational expectations and emotional bias.

AI is undoubtedly a macro-trend that opens the possibility for immense value creation by companies. But not all that would glitter is gold. Not all companies will be in a position to effectively cash in on the opportunity and translate it into sustainable value creation for stakeholders. A rising tide can initially raise all the boats. However, the competition would be intense. Only the leading players with cutting-edge technology, the best talent, expertise, strategic intent, and solid corporate governance would emerge winners in the long term. Remember that merely a handful of large companies could survive the dot-com crisis and thrived afterward to become the eBays and Amazons of today.

Even though AI is a highly promising technology, not all AI-based products will be commercially successful. Over the years, we have seen many extremely hyped products like VR headsets, wearable technologies like Google Glass, and Hoverboards that failed to deliver on the high promises. Since AI is an evolving space with a myriad of potential applications, the number of investment avenues would be very large. This increases the need for careful due diligence before making investments.

The AI space is increasingly intensifying with a huge interest from institutional investors, a media frenzy, and a gold rush by retail investors. We can only expect a higher frequency launches of new AI applications, product categories, and specialized AI companies. There will also be entries of fly-by-night firms looking to make a fortune riding the AI fever. Existing firms would increasingly mention AI in their quarterly earnings reports. Don't be surprised at new firms slapping AI to their names to increase valuations or crypto folks flocking to the AI space to create speculative bubbles. We can already see AI-related crypto tokens like Fetch (FET), SingularityNET (AGIX), and Ocean Protocol (OCEAN) appreciating rapidly. So, what's cooking? Is it another bubble in making? Possibly, yes!

Along with Newton, there was another famous person who invested in the South Sea Company in the early days. Similar to Newton, he also made an early exit from the stocks and made an even bigger fortune - a profit of about £175,000. However, unlike the great physicist, he refrained from re-investing in the stock when the price was already too high. Rather, Thomas Guy, a British bookseller and member of parliament. used the money to build Guy's Hospital which continues to contribute towards clinical research to this day.

Investing does not always require a creative genius - more often, it needs patience, commonsense, and control of one's emotions.

KEY TAKEAWAYS

- Market bubbles occur due to a rapid increase in the price of an asset in a short period, followed by a rapid decline, usually driven by greed, enthusiasm, and herd mentality with little consideration for the underlying company fundamentals.
- The four stages of a market bubble are the stealth phase, awareness phase, mania phase, and blow-off phase. Historical market bubbles include the Tulip mania, Dot-com bubble, and the US housing market bubble.
- You need to learn from these past examples and avoid emotional bias while investing in megatrends like AI. Although AI is a highly promising technology, not all AI-based products will be commercially successful. Conduct due diligence before buying stocks and consider factors like the company's moat, competitive advantages and financial position

Chapter 6

STAGES OF TECHNOLOGY ADOPTION - ENTHUSIASTS, LAGGARDS, AND THE MAJORITY IN BETWEEN

Once a new technology rolls over you, if you're not part of the steamroller, you're part of the road.
- Stewart Brand

One million iPhones in 74 days! exclaimed Apple's legendary CEO Steve Jobs in a newly released press note. It was the second week of September 2007. 2.5 months back Apple launched its first iPhone - arguably the most successful technology product to date. The initial sale was mainly supported by innovators and early adopters - technology enthusiasts who were the first ones to grab a new innovation.

15 years later, Apple sold 225 million iPhones in 2022 which equates to one million iPhones flying off the shelves every 36 hours! The iPhone is no more a product coveted by only a few technology fans - it has assumed mass adoption through different stages of technology adoption.

The transition from one technology to another does not happen overnight. Celebrated management Guru Peter Drucker once famously said - *for new technology to replace old, it has to have at least ten times the benefit.*

Whenever a new technology arrives, there're always apprehensions or even resistance to change. The benefits and the promises of the new technology need to be materially high. In most cases, a very small number of early buyers, the more adventurous ones, try a novel technology in the initial days. Their positive experience, feedback, and words of mouth often trigger the next round of much wider adoption. However, when a product fails to impress early buyers, more often than not it fades into gradual oblivion. Last few decades we have seen that for every invention like the iPhone that assumes the cult figure, there're many more products like the much-hyped Google Glass that ultimately fail.

A repeated theme we would like to reiterate in this book is that AI is a groundbreaking technology that can disrupt the entire business world. However, will all businesses and individual users adopt AI applications as soon as they are introduced? The answer is an obvious no. Every user would have its own risk-reward parameters to decide when to adopt certain technology and to what extent. How is it going to benefit me? - this is the most vital question a user would ask for.

We can already observe certain highly futuristic and technology-driven firms adopting AI at a higher rate than others. Moving forward, more firms would adopt these applications as the benefits become more visible and obvious. There would still be some laggards who would wait till the very last moment until they are almost forced to adopt AI faced with an existential crisis. However, a large majority of firms will adopt AI applications between the early adopter stage and the laggards stage.

Why does the adoption rate of new technologies almost always follow a standard template? Let's explore.

Technology adoption curve

The mass transition from basic mobile phones to smartphones took about a decade. It's not a big deal anymore to convince someone about the benefits of having a smartphone. Now, what about EVs?

While the most environmentally-conscious consumers with a bigger budget are ditching their fuel guzzlers for the pricier EVs, they are yet to be a mass-market product. However, it's fairly safe to assume that EVs will be adopted at a much faster rate with declining prices and improving performance. Now think about a VR headset. Would it really have any serious takers unless the metaverse becomes something as big as the social media of today?

Any new technology, be it a smartphone or a VR headset, generally goes through the technology adoption curve over its useful life. This is a bell-shaped curve depicting how new technologies are adopted by different users over their lifetime. The curve shows five stages of technology adoption.

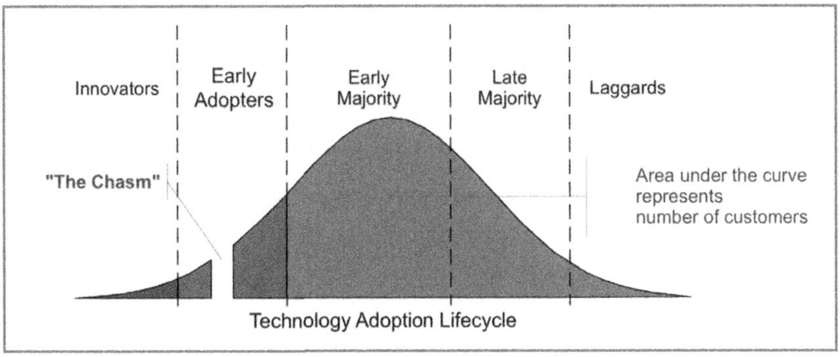

Figure 9: *The technology adoption lifecycle (source: Wikimedia Commons)*

Stage 1: Innovators

We've been in line for days, Melanie Rivera, a visibly excited customer queueing outside Apple's SoHo store in New York City, told CNN Money. She added - *It's very uncomfortable out here in these chairs. But people are very social. We've made it through the rain, so we feel like we're getting closer to the phone.* It was June 29, 2007 - Apple's much-awaited iPhone was available in the stores for the first time.

Melanie is the perfect example of an innovator who is always on the look out for the next technological innovation and grabs it before the majority. Generally, innovators constitute a very small percentage (typically about 2.5%) of the total consumers. They are ready to assume risks (the new product may not be good enough) and pay a higher price as new inventions are generally priced higher in the beginning. In the case of AI, the innovators are the firms that could foretell the massive future applications of AI based on the data revolution in the last two decades.

Stage 2: Early adopters

They constitute about 13.5% of the total consumers. Early adopters are often called opinion leaders because their opinion and experience greatly influence the further adoption of the product. They generally have a great understanding of new technologies and how to exploit the same to fulfill a long-term strategic vision.

What differentiates the early adopters from the innovators is that the former first evaluate the new technology for its long-term potential rather than just rushing to try any emerging technology. Firms like Google, Amazon, Apple, and IBM can be counted as early adopters of AI as they made the first moves to commercially exploit AI.

Stage 3: Early majority

This stage of technology adoption is reached when the early adopters have started deriving benefits from the new technology. The early majority of users generally wait and watch the developments in the market without committing resources to new technologies. They devise their adoption strategy only after the early adopters are serious about the technology. The early majority of users, take calculated steps in technology adoption by learning from others' experiences.

Early majority users constitute around 34% of total users. According to IBM's AI Adoption Index 2022, 35% of companies are already using some form of AI while an additional 42% of firms are actively exploring AI. Given these statistics, we can safely assume that AI adoption has already reached the early majority stage. Large firms (early adopters) are making huge investments in it while many smaller counterparts are taking calculated steps.

Stage 4: Late majority

These users are first skeptical about new technology, but start adopting it when a majority is already walking the same path. The late majority firms constitute 34% of total consumers, the same as the early majority. These firms are mostly risk-averse. They would commit resources only when the market is ripe and they would be left behind if they don't act now. The mass adoption of a technology takes place when it reaches the late majority stage.

AI adoption is costly. Firms need to invest in costly computational capacity, hire AI professionals, and disrupt their core business processes to integrate AI. These are costly bets. Risk-averse firms would like to wait until AI becomes mainstream. We can expect AI to reach the late majority stage by the end of this decade.

Stage 5: Laggards

These users are generally indifferent to new technology. They are the least interested and they are the last ones to adopt new technology. However, it's not a small user base - around 1 in 6 users is a laggard - a whopping 16% of the total users.

Laggards are generally conservative and like to maintain the status quo. Since they are not very comfortable with technological changes, laggards adopt new technology only when they absolutely have to. Since AI is a rapidly progressing technology, the laggards face the risk of extinction in a highly competitive business environment.

Factors affecting the rate of technology adoption

The technology adoption lifecycle gives a simplified and standard view of how technology progresses from its introduction to maturity. However, in real life, things are not always that simple. Technologies are hardly static. The first-generation smartphones are not the same as the ones we use today. The features and performance have improved drastically with new innovations coming almost every year. Similarly, AI is an evolving technology with a plethora of applications that would have their own life cycles. Therefore, technology adoption does not always happen in a linear or predictable bell curve fashion. There can be faster, slower, a sudden surge, or even a sudden halt in adoption based on various factors. The wired telephone that served as the communication lifeline for the first world countries never became mainstream in many developing countries.

Let's look at some important factors that affect technology adoption:

Innovation

Rapid innovation can make technology adoption faster. Rapid smartphone innovations - be it in drastic improvements in the camera or rapidly increased internal memory, have expedited their adoption rate. Moreover, innovations in related domains can also make technology more desirable. Rapid progress in the e-commerce industry has invariably increased demand for smartphones - especially among first-time users. Similarly, AI would be adopted more rapidly when new innovations add value to the users.

Supporting infrastructure

Would smartphones be as popular and widely used had we not moved from 2G to 4G or even 5G technologies? Why buy an electric car if there're not enough charging stations? In fact, one of the vital factors behind the relatively slower adoption of EVs in countries like India, Brazil, and Indonesia is the lack of charging infrastructure.

Improvement in infrastructure gives a rapid push to related technologies. AI applications may require gigantic computing power. Also, there's a substantial skill gap that can be fulfilled by training people on these technologies using an efficient educational infrastructure. Moreover, government support in building an enabling infrastructure would be crucial for the growth of AI - especially in developing countries.

Differentiation

Users don't have a homogenous need. For technology to penetrate deeper into the market, it needs to meet the varied needs of different users. While cost reduction can be the primary goal of a firm, another may be looking to convert more customer queries into sales.

The differentiation ability of a technology affects its adoption rate. You can use a smartphone to shop online or stay connected with friends and family while someone else can use it primarily for entertainment - for say watching Netflix. Similarly, AI's future adoption rate would depend on how AI firms can differentiate their offerings to create value for different users. The wider the value creation, the faster would be its adoption rate.

KEY TAKEAWAYS

- Technology adoption follows a bell-shaped curve with five stages: Innovators, Early Adopters, Early Majority, Late Majority, and Laggards. AI adoption is currently at the Early Majority stage and we can expected it to reach the Late Majority stage by the end of the decade.
- Factors affecting technology adoption rates include the pace of innovation, supporting infrastructure, and differentiation.
- For individual investors, understanding the technology adoption curve and the factors affecting adoption rates can help you make informed decisions about investing in companies that develop, use, or benefit from AI and other emerging technologies.

Chapter 7

THE TWO KEY AI INVESTING THEMES - HARDWARE AND SOFTWARE

Investing in tomorrow's technology today is more critical than ever
- Bill Gates.

In 1965 American engineer Gordon Moore, who later co-founded Intel, made an interesting observation - the number of transistors on a microchip doubles almost every two years while the costs halved. For the uninitiated, this means the processing power of computers is predicted to rise constantly at this rate with falling costs. Over the years, this observation has come to be known as *Moore's Law* serving as a benchmark for computational advancement. In the last few decades, *Moor's Law* has been more refined and the doubling period has fallen to nearly 14-18 months with rapid innovation in computing. Then came the AI - a different beast altogether.

AI researcher Jaime Sevilla, along with his colleagues at the University of Aberdeen, tracked the performance of AI systems from 1959 to 2022. The team observed that between 1959 and 2010, processing power to train AI applications doubled around every 17-29 months. This was nearly at the pace predicted by *Moore's Law*. Then with the advancement of deep learning (a subset of machine learning) growth rate of AI-related computing power went up drastically - doubling around every 4 to 9 months. Stanford University's AI Index 2019 showed even more astounding progress - AI computing power doubling every 3.4 months!

AI is now powered by much more supplicated hardware and software than traditional computer systems.

The race for futuristic hardware and software

AI has been made possible because of a confluence of the holy trinity - advanced computing (hardware), the availability of large volumes of data, and sophisticated algorithms (software) like machine learning. The leading AI companies have long realized that they need a broad mix of technological capabilities including hardware and software to exploit AI's market potential.

CPU, GPU, FPGA, and ASIC

The design of modern computers we see today is mainly based on the computer architecture of the 1940s given by computer scientist and mathematician John von Neumann. In this design, data processing takes place in the Central Processing Unit (CPU) whereas data and programs are located in separate hardware called memory. This arrangement has worked great so far. But, rapid progress in artificial intelligence exposed its shortcomings - it cannot efficiently generate the humongous computing power needed for AI.

Since there's a physical partition between the CPU and memory, data needs to be shuttled back and forth between these two hardware components. AI techniques, especially deep learning (a branch of machine learning), require faster and more energy-efficient computing. Hardware designers are looking for alternate designs. What's a better place to find one than the human brain, the most efficient information-processing system in nature?

Companies like IBM are working to build alternative architectures like in-memory computing (IMC). Instead of having separate hardware for processing and memory, in IMC processing takes place within the memory itself. We have also seen in recent years AI computing depending heavily on Graphics Processing Units (GPUs) - a shift from traditional CPUs. GPUs are better suited for parallel processing and multitasking. Rather than sequential processing in CPUs, a GPU breaks down tasks to process sub-tasks parallelly. This makes GPUs a preferred vehicle for various specialized AI models, creating a huge windfall gain for companies like Nvidia which is the uncontested leader in GPU production. The company has successfully utilized its video-gaming experience to become one of the leading AI companies of today.

In addition to GPU, the other emerging technologies in the processing space are Field Programmable Gate Arrays (FPGAs) and Application-Specific Integrated Circuits (ASICs). FPGAs and ASICs are highly customizable processors that can suit specific applications.

AI - a new goldmine for chip makers

Apart from advanced computer architecture, AI needs specialized microprocessors that can run AI applications smoothly. Leading semiconductor companies like IBM, Intel, and AMD are expanding their facilities and investing heavily in R&D to stay ahead in the race. With the rapid proliferation of AI applications, chip makers wouldn't only face increased demand for existing chips but also for special-purpose microprocessors to meet specific needs.

The AI microprocessor market size was estimated at $10.25 billion in 2021. According to a Mckinsey report, AI can generate $85-$95 billion in revenue for chip manufacturers by 2025.

AI software - programs that run AI applications

AI software is the algorithms or computer programs that use machine learning to execute intelligent functions like speech recognition or image generation. AI software is supported by advanced hardware enabling developers to build various AI applications that suit specific user requirements. Therefore, AI software development is a vast space that can accommodate boundless innovation and creativity. While the AI hardware market may be dominated by a few large players because of their resourcefulness and expertise, the AI software market opens a floodgate for a large number of start-ups and emerging players. According to Precedence Research, the global AI software market was estimated to be $138.4 billion in 2022.

Leading AI hardware companies

Nvidia

The graphics giant made its foray into AI with full force around 2015-16. In April 2020, Nvidia acquired computer networking company Mellanox Technologies for $7 billion. This acquisition greatly enhanced Nvidia's AI capabilities through faster networking performance. Nvidia is the market leader in GPU computing and one of the leading companies in the AI space. Nvidia is aiming at 1,000X processing speed through GPU computing by 2025. In addition to hardware, Nvidia is a major contender for the AI software market as well.

Intel

The largest semiconductor company by revenue, Intel is investing heavily to gear up its AI capabilities. In 2019, Intel acquired AI chipmaker Habana Labs for $2 billion to substantially increase its AI arsenal. The very next year, Intel invested another $132 million in 11 startups related to AI and automation. In 2022, it acquired AI-based startup Granulate for $650 million, making its aggressive expansion plans in AI very obvious.

AMD

It's a major global chip maker with a 30% market share in the overall CPU market in Q4 2022. In May 2022, AMD bought Pensando Systems for $1.9 billion to solidify its leadership in Data Processing Units (DPUs). The same year, AMD acquired semiconductor manufacturer Xilinx in a record $49 billion deal. The acquisition greatly enhanced AMD's capabilities in adaptive computing to exploit the AI market.

Google

Over the last two decades, Google has become synonymous with the term search engine. However, in 2016 its new CEO Sundar Pichai vowed to make Google an AI-first company. 2 years back in 2014, Google acquired London-based AI startup DeepMind for more than $500 million. It was a significant move towards making Google an AI-based company. Even though Google is not traditionally known as a hardware company, it has significant dominance in the AI hardware market with its AI-specific products like Tensor Processing Unit (TPU).

IBM

It's one of the legacy players in the AI hardware market with its supercomputer Watson being one of the earliest demonstrations of intelligent machines. The AI Hardware Center at IBM has developed a specialized computer chip for AI called Artificial Intelligence Unit (AIU). It's an ASIC that can be programmed to handle any deep-learning task. IBM's AI Hardware Center is fully dedicated to advancing holistic technologies in this space. The company aims at training and running AI models 1,000 times faster by 2029 compared to 2019.

In addition to these established market players, there're some highly promising startups like Cerebras Systems, Graphcore, and SambaNova which can make it big in the AI hardware segment. These startups are building next-generation chips customized for the AI industry.

Leading AI software companies

Microsoft

For decades, Microsoft has enjoyed a near-monopoly status in Operating Systems. Currently, it's the hottest player in the AI software segment with the recent integration of its search engine Bing with ChatGPT. In 2019, Microsoft invested $1 billion in OpenAI, the company behind

ChapGPT. In January 2023, Microsoft committed another $10 billion investment in OpenAI to greatly enhance its AI prowess.

OpenAI

It's one of the leading limited-profit AI research labs. OpenAI was founded in 2015 with serial entrepreneur Elon Musk being one of the co-founders. Currently valued at $29 billion, OpenAI is heavily funded by Microsoft. Over the last few years, OpenAI has developed some groundbreaking AI models like ChatGPT, GPT-3, DALL-E, and Whisper (speech recognition system).

Google

The search engine leader is one of the top contenders in the AI software space with its vast experience in developing the best algorithms and cutting-edge technology. Google recently released Bard, its conversational AI and a rival of ChatGPT, demonstrating its advancement in AI software development. Even though the product is at an experimental stage and its release was quite botched up (Bard gave a wrong answer in a featured Ad), the technological capability of Google cannot be underestimated. Moreover, Google's DeepMind has already developed sophisticated AI applications like AlphaFold (predicts protein structure) and AlphaGO (gaming application).

Meta

The social networking giant is one of the leaders in the AI race. Back in 2013, its CEO Mark Zuckerberg made it a mission to transform the company into an AI leader. Over the years, Meta has invested billions of dollars in AI research and development. Even though Meta has a deep focus on the immersive technology called metaverse (this is also one of the reasons the company got its new name), it would be interesting to see how AI is integrated into this technology in the coming years.

Apple

With a current market valuation of over $2.4 trillion, Apple is the most valuable publicly traded company in the world. Apple is known for developing marvelous technology products like the iPhone, iPod, and Apple Watch. Apple has been successfully integrating AI applications like Siri (natural language processing) and Face ID (image recognition) with its products to create a world-class customer experience.

KEY TAKEAWAYS

- ◇ AI advancements significantly outpace Moore's Law, requiring alternative computer architectures and specialized hardware for efficient processing.
- ◇ Major companies like Nvidia, Intel, AMD, Google, and IBM dominate the AI hardware market, while the AI software market offers opportunities for start-ups and emerging players.
- ◇ The AI microprocessor market and global AI software market present massive growth potential, driving investments and innovations across the industry.

Chapter 8

7 STOCKS FOR THE AI REVOLUTION

In this chapter we'll be highlighting 7 companies which we believe are best situated to benefit from AI in the medium to long term. This is not a recommendation to buy them at any price, and you must consider the stock's intrinsic value. If that's an area you're not familiar with, you can get our free Valuation 101 course by going to

https://freemanpublications.com/bonus

One more thing, we're listing the companies in alphabetical order, not in order of best-to-worst investment potential.

So let's get cracking...

Amazon: A Long-Term Story

Amazon (AMZN) has fallen from a high of about $180 in July 2021 to $100 as of February 8, 2023. That is a massive fall of 56%. We believe that this correction presents a solid opportunity for long-term investors because AMZN is innovating by incorporating AI into every sphere of its business. Thereby setting the company up for the next growth phase, which is likely to start by mid-2023 after the Fed signals that it is done with hiking interest rates.

Figure 10: *Amazon price between February 2020 and February 2023 (Source: Trading View)*

Here are our reasons why we consider AMZN to deliver superior gains in the long term:

A. The Recent Price Crash Is Irrational

Income Statement (Quarterly)

Financials in millions USD. Fiscal year is January - December.

Quarter Ended	2022-12-31	2022-09-30	2022-06-30	2022-03-31
Revenue	**149,204**	**127,101**	**121,234**	**116,444**
Revenue Growth (YoY)	8.58%	14.70%	7.21%	7.30%
Cost of Revenue	85,640	70,268	66,424	66,499
Gross Profit	**63,564**	**56,833**	**54,810**	**49,945**
Selling, General & Admin	16,151	14,075	12,989	10,914
Research & Development	20,814	19,485	18,072	14,842
Other Operating Expenses	23,862	20,748	20,432	20,520
Operating Expenses	60,827	54,308	51,493	46,276
Operating Income	**2,737**	**2,525**	**3,317**	**3,669**

Figure 11: *Amazon Income Statement for the previous 4 quarters (Source: stockanalysis.com)*

In Q4 2022, AMZN reported an operating income of $2.7 billion, which was 21% lower year over year ($3.46 billion in Q4 2021). Investors quickly latched on to this lower number and hammered the stock without paying heed to the events that lowered the operating income.

Specifically, three significant and non-recurring expenses worth $2.7 billion were responsible for this decrease:

1. Employee severance.
2. An increase in impairments to property, plant, and equipment. In Q4 2022, AMZN provided for $12.5 billion worth of impairments compared to $10 billion, quarter over quarter.
3. Changes in estimated self-insurance liabilities.

If these items were not present, the company would have reported an operating income of $5.4 billion versus $3.46 billion in Q4 2021. The big takeaway is that by laying off people and providing for other expenses or impairments (a non-cash charge), AMZN has solidly improved its profitability potential and made its balance sheet more robust! Things can only get better from here on.

We believe the market has gone overboard, hammering AMZN to its current levels.

B. AMZN's Focus On AI

We all know that AI is already upon us and will likely change how our lives go forward. We have already witnessed how MSFT/OpenAI's ChatGPT and GOOG's Bard AI create waves immediately after their introduction. AMZN too is very big on AI, but its presence is not as visible as the tools mentioned above. Specifically, here is how AMZN is incorporating AI into its e-commerce operations, both online and offline:

1. AMZN prompts its shoppers with options such as "Customers Also Bought" and "Recommended For You." AMZN's AI engine extracts these recommendations/suggestions, and such prompts help the company increase sales. The AI engine analyses the user's search

history, shopping history, items in their cart, and viewed items.

2. Of course, AMZN's search bar gives amazing and relevant recommendations on the fly (as soon as the shopper starts keying in the search terms) – and this, too, is enabled by AMZN's powerful AI engine.

3. AMZN's AI allows Alexa/Echo users to conveniently buy products by speaking to the device – there is no need to touch any screen. This intelligent voice-enabled shopping is available in 15 languages across 80 countries.

4. AMZN also uses AI in its warehouses to ensure optimal inventory levels, optimize delivery routes, predict demand per state/geography, track supply chains, and more. This is why the company has been able to introduce its one-day shipping/delivery feature. AI will also enable drone deliveries soon.

5. AMZN's AI also helped the company launch its Go brand of convenience stores, where customers can self-checkout without interacting with human cashiers. There is no waiting in line and billing is done through the AMZN app, thanks to AI.

C. AMZN's Financials

Cash Flow Statement (Quarterly)

Financials in millions USD. Fiscal year is January - December.

Quarter Ended	2022-12-31	2022-09-30	2022-06-30	2022-03-31
Net Income	**278**	**2,872**	**-2,028**	**-3,844**
Depreciation & Amortization	13,145	10,204	9,594	8,978
Share-Based Compensation	5,606	5,556	5,209	3,250
Other Operating Activities	10,144	-7,228	-3,810	-11,174
Operating Cash Flow	**29,173**	**11,404**	**8,965**	**-2,790**
Operating Cash Flow Growth	32.09%	55.94%	-29.49%	-
Capital Expenditures	-15,440	-15,041	-14,098	-13,742
Acquisitions	-831	-885	-259	-6,341
Change in Investments	5,450	318	2,279	20,989
Investing Cash Flow	**-10,821**	**-15,608**	**-12,078**	**906**
Share Issuance / Repurchase	0	0	-3,334	-2,666
Debt Issued / Paid	86	3,016	7,960	4,656
Other Financing Activities	-	-	-	-
Financing Cash Flow	**86**	**3,016**	**4,626**	**1,990**
Net Cash Flow	**19,075**	**-2,522**	**1,101**	**122**
Free Cash Flow	13,733	-3,637	-5,133	-16,532

Figure 12: *Amazon Cash Flow Statement for the previous 4 quarters (Source: stockanalysis.com)*

In Q4 2022, AMZN generated solid operating cash flows worth $29 billion because of higher amortization and working capital adjustments. It represented an increase of 32% year over year, and a rise of 156%, quarter over quarter. This humongous cash flow generation was ignored entirely by investors – along with the fact that AMZN reported a lower operating and net income because of the three significant and non-recurring expenses discussed in Section A above.

We believe the growth will be slow for the next couple of quarters because of global economic uncertainty and recession in the EU. AMZN's management says shoppers are becoming more cautious and reducing their discretionary spending. We are all aware that economic cycles come and go and that recessions slowly turn into booms and vice versa. When the tide turns, know that AMZN is present in 180 countries, has 300+ million active users, and 2 million selling partners worldwide. Sales and profits can grow exponentially as the tide turns.

The company is also hooking new users to its Amazon Prime platform. In 2022, the company invested $7 billion to create and license content on Amazon Prime. The management believes that the Prime platform will continue to increase its member engagement and new user acquisition.

Of the $149 billion revenues generated in Q4 2022, about $21 billion came from AWS. The management believes that AWS, too, will witness an increase in revenues because many enterprises are transitioning to the cloud. AWS is backed by a robust AI engine that automates workflow, analyzes images/content, detects problems, personalizes user experience, forecasts business metrics, and more.

The company's balance sheet, worth $462 billion, is highly robust. Of the total balance sheet, AMZN owns hard (non-intangible) long-term assets worth $285 billion and cash and short-term investments worth $70 billion. Long-term debt is just $74 billion, or about 50% of the common equity, at $146 billion as of December 2022.

Summing Up

We believe that AMZN has solid long-term potential and is one AI pioneer that investors are ignoring. Investors are looking at the short term and dumping the stock because it has reported lower profits in Q4 2022 – without going into the reasons. They are neither paying attention to how AMZN is revolutionizing the shopping experience by injecting AI into our shopping lives nor are they paying attention to AMZN's solid financials and exciting prospects.

We also believe that the Fed will keep increasing rates, and we estimate that rates will likely peak at 5.25% by mid-2023. Until then, the market will be gingery. But then, we are calling AMZN a long-term coffee can stock – therefore, this recommendation is purely for patient long-term investors interested in buying solid value and growth stocks.

Google: Dive Into The Dip

A minor and potentially inconsequential error by Alphabet's Bard AI, which is still under development, sent investors into a bearish frenzy. They responded by hammering Alphabet (GOOG) down from about $109 to its current low of about $95.

***Figure 13:** Google price between November 2022 and February 2023 (Source: Trading View)*

For some short sellers and panicked investors, the world had ended for GOOG and the company had no future. We believe these investors are behaving irrationally and making a massive mistake by dumping GOOG, which has just begun its AI journey.

We believe that GOOG has tremendous potential, and here are our reasons why it is a coffee-can portfolio stock:

New and Exciting Developments at GOOG

- GOOG latched on to AI over 6 years ago and is considered one of the pioneers of AI. Most generative AI applications today are based on GOOG's Transformer Project, a novel neural network focused on modeling languages, machine translation, and answering questions. Barn AI is still under development and it is a huge mistake to write off a stock based on one minor error made by a new application still under development.
- GOOG is also in the advanced stages of completing LaMDA – a chatbot system that analyzes very advanced large language models around the world – and PaLM (Pathways Language Model), an AI architecture that can easily handle millions of tasks, including reasoning. PaLM has so far outperformed the most sophisticated language models and humans in tests of reasoning and language.
- GOOG has already deployed a neural network like BERT (Bidirectional Encoder Representations from Transformers) in its search engine to interpret a searcher's intentions. It understands words, idioms, content, and phrases as humans do. GOOG has also deployed MUM (Multitask Unified Model) in its search engine. MUM works by understanding the searcher's context and delivering search results that improve his search experience.
- The best thing is that all the technologies described above are being improved upon as you read this. If you visualize the future of search and online surfing experience with all these technologies, you will perceive that your device will interact with you just like a know-it-all and wise human would!
- GOOG also provides these AI technologies in its cloud and will soon offer APIs to individuals and businesses to innovate and create more cutting-edge experiences for online users. One example worth mentioning is that GOOG's DeepMind (an AI company of scientists, engineers, and researchers) offers a protein database containing 200 million proteins. The database is used by 1 million biologists and is enabled by GOOG's AI.

GOOG's Growing Usage

- YouTube Shorts witnessed a massive jump in its subscribers in 2022. It averaged 50 billion daily views in Q4 2022, up from 30 billion daily views logged in Q1 2022. The numbers are growing as we write this because YouTube has begun sharing revenues with content providers.
- YouTube Music (Premium) crossed 80 million subscribers in Q4 2022.
- GOOG's cloud revenues grew 32%, year over year. GOOG provides its cloud users with real-time data, incisive analytics, and AI, which helps GOOG's cloud analyze 110+ terabytes of data per second. GOOG's supercomputers and AI tools help customers like Kroger analyze data across different services and customers like Snap triple their workload at a lower cost. GOOG's cloud customer list is growing and many majors like Bayer, Calico, Weibo, and more are discovering a lot of value in it.

GOOG's Financials

GOOG's revenues and net income took a hit in Q4 2022 because of the Fed's high interest rate regime, an appreciating dollar, and the general macroeconomic uncertainty, which led to lower ad spending. These adverse developments made the company miss its quarterly EPS guidance by $0.15. The guidance miss was followed up by the Bard AI error, which panicked the investors.

However, GOOG's profitability is the gold standard. We believe that aside from these short-term hiccups, the company is set to break its previous profitability records with all its leading-edge AI tools.

	Sector Relative Grade	GOOG	Sector Median
Gross Profit Margin (TTM)	B-	55.38%	49.63%
EBIT Margin (TTM)	A+	26.46%	9.32%
EBITDA Margin (TTM)	A-	32.09%	18.78%
Net Income Margin (TTM)	A+	21.20%	3.34%
Levered FCF Margin (TTM)	A-	18.57%	8.88%
Return on Common Equity (TTM)	A+	23.62%	3.62%
Return on Total Capital (TTM)	A+	16.52%	3.54%
Return on Total Assets (TTM)	A+	16.42%	1.68%
CAPEX / Sales (TTM)	B+	11.13%	3.90%
Asset Turnover Ratio (TTM)	B+	0.78x	0.47x
Cash From Operations (TTM)	A+	91.49B	210.42M
Net Income Per Employee (TTM)	A+	315.25K	10.99K

Figure 14: *Google profitability metrics vs. sector peers (Source: Seeking Alpha)*

A hefty gross profit margin of 55.38% (sector median: 49.63%), a solid 16.42% return on total assets (sector median 1.68%), and a net income of $315K per employee (sector median: $10.99K) suggest that the company is highly profitable and very efficiently managed by a team that is one step ahead of the competition (well, ChatGPT was a one-off).

For the record, with a balance sheet of $365 billion, GOOG owns cash and short-term investments worth $114 billion. About 31% of GOOG's balance sheet is held in liquid assets and with such a massive war chest, the company can afford to acquire competitors and startups and thereby make a vast difference in the market. GOOG's long-term debt is just $13 billion compared to its total common equity of $256 billion. The company's balance sheet is more robust than one can imagine.

Summing Up

No serious investor would dump GOOG because the company missed its guidance for one quarter or because Barn AI made one minor error.

GOOG is a long-term portfolio pick mainly because its enterprise AI architecture innovations are set to start paying off in the near term. Plus, the gains from its R&D are likely to flow in for decades – just like they did when GOOG launched its search engine.

The company's profitability is the best out there; investors must be patient with the stock. There may be a few downers until the Fed signals that the interest rate hikes are done with, but such events should be of no consequence to a serious long-term investor.

We are bullish on GOOG and believe the current dip represents a fantastic entry point for long-term investors.

Intel: Take Advantage Of Near-Term Headwinds

Intel (INTC) has taken a knock since its price registered a post-COVID high of about $69. The Fed's interest rate hikes, coupled with recessionary fears, have led to the hammering of technology stocks, pushing the price down. We believe that the current investor disinterest in INTC can be taken advantage of by patient investors who believe in AI's power to change how we live, interact and do business.

Figure 15: *Intel price chart between 2015 and 2023 (Source: Trading View)*

INTC is currently hovering around $28, and its long-term support level is pegged at about $25. We believe that the stock makes for a solid long-term investment. Here are our reasons why:

1. INTC Leverages AI

The company creates software and hardware that help users extract efficiently and productively the best possible outcome from their AI applications. INTC also equips its users with open-source tools and other tools that enable end-to-end machine learning.

Now, when you are thinking about AI, you need to visualize the following: autonomous cars, AI-powered robots that work in factories, AI-enabled healthcare that accurately diagnoses diseases, speed up drug discovery, helps provide virtual (instructive) medical aid, and analyzes data to create solutions for a healthier world, AI-powered customer service robots, and many more.

Almost every sector out there needs AI and many have already begun transitioning to it. It is just a matter of time before AI becomes all-pervasive and INTC reaps the benefits.

2. The Company is Cutting Costs

INTC's management is focused on cutting costs by $3 billion in 2023 and up to $23 billion by the end of 2025. The costs would be cut by laying off people, enforcing unpaid leaves, exiting unprofitable verticals, and more – well, these are desperate times and such times call for desperate measures. This saving will help the company wipe out its losses and return to its earlier profitable ways in 2023.

Earnings from Continuing Operations	Dec 2022	Oct 2022	Jul 2022	Apr 2022
Interest Expense	(149.0)	(114.0)	(109.0)	(124.0)
Interest And Investment Income	274.0	170.0	98.0	47.0
Net Interest Expenses	125.0	56.0	(11.0)	(77.0)
Currency Exchange Gains (Loss)	(460.0)	771.0	1,023.0	158.0
Other Non Operating Income (Expenses)	1,557.0	(689.0)	(1,131.0)	(205.0)
EBT, Incl. Unusual Items	(796.0)	(188.0)	(909.0)	9,661.0
Income Tax Expense	(135.0)	(1,207.0)	(455.0)	1,548.0
Earnings From Continuing Operations	**(661.0)**	**1,019.0**	**(454.0)**	**8,113.0**

Figure 16: *Intel Cash Flow statement for the previous 4 quarters (Source: Seeking Alpha)*

In Q4 2022, the company reported a net loss of $661 million because of various factors. These included the impact of the Russia–Ukraine war on the global economy, economic uncertainty, rising interest rates, recession in the EU, and the recent COVID-related shutdown in China (In 2021, China contributed 21% to INTC's revenues). These factors dealt a severe blow to the PC market and weakened it considerably. The company expects the economic weakness to persist in H1 2023 and bounce back after that.

So, the worst-case scenario is that INTC will end up incurring a $2.64 billion loss in 2023 ($661 loss/quarter), which will get wholly offset by its cost savings of $3 billion, resulting in a small profit.

In the best-case scenario, INTC will incur a loss of $1.32 billion ($661 loss/quarter) in H1 2023, and some profit that is currently difficult to estimate in H2 2023. After accounting for cost savings of $3 billion in 2023, the company will have a healthy net income that should please the investors.

3. New Developments at INTC

- ◇ Though INTC's H2 2022 sales were muted, the company grew its share in the PC market – plus, it expects the positive momentum to continue into 2023.
- ◇ The company's share in the server market grew at a modest rate. Hyperscale servers saw a jump in sales, but the demand for enterprise servers declined because of the company's exposure to China. The company expects growth to pick up in H2 2023.
- ◇ The automotive, industrial, and infrastructure trends were strong in 2022 but were somewhat impacted by the macroeconomic factors discussed above.
- ◇ Intel witnessed an increase in demand for its products and services supplied by its NEX (Networking and Edge Group) and Mobileye Global (autonomous driving technologies and advanced driver-assistance systems (ADAS)) business divisions.
- ◇ The company's focus on R&D helped it introduce the 4th gen Xeon scalable CPU and Xeon CPU MAX series on January 10, 2023. INTC estimates it will ship 1 million units of these chips by H1 2023. INTC's DCAI (Data Center and AI Group) is sampling a cutting-edge server processor (Emerald Rapids) and is on track to launch it in H2 2023. INTC is also on track to launch two new AI-enabling, edgy processors (Granite Rapids and Sierra Forest) in 2024.

4. A Robust Balance Sheet

	Last Report	Dec 2022	Dec 2021	Dec 2020	Dec 2019
Cash & Short Term Investments					
Cash And Equivalents	11,144.0	11,144.0	4,827.0	5,865.0	4,194.0
Short Term Investments	17,194.0	17,194.0	24,426.0	2,292.0	1,082.0
Trading Asset Securities	-	-	-	15,738.0	7,847.0
Total Cash & ST Investments	**28,338.0**	**28,338.0**	**29,253.0**	**23,895.0**	**13,123.0**
Receivables					
Accounts Receivable	4,133.0	4,133.0	9,457.0	6,782.0	7,659.0
Other Receivables	138.0	138.0	23.0	131.0	76.0
Total Receivables	**4,324.0**	**4,324.0**	**9,632.0**	**7,352.0**	**7,735.0**
Current Assets					
Inventory	13,224.0	13,224.0	10,776.0	8,427.0	8,744.0
Deferred Tax Assets Current	-	-	-	-	-
Other Current Assets	4,521.0	4,521.0	8,897.0	7,575.0	1,637.0
Total Current Assets	**50,407.0**	**50,407.0**	**58,558.0**	**47,249.0**	**31,239.0**

Figure 17: *Intel Balance Sheet for the previous 4 years (Source: Seeking Alpha)*

INTC owns liquid assets (cash and short-term investments) worth $28 billion and fast-moving inventories worth $13 billion in a balance sheet of $182 billion – the company has more than sufficient cash to take advantage of any disruption in the market, pay dividends, and tide over troubled times. Plus, retained earnings of $70 billion supplement the company's common stock worth $31.6 billion. INTC's long-term debt is $37.7 billion, which works out to just 37% of the company's total equity.

5. INTC is Cheaply Valued

	Sector Relative Grade	INTC	Sector Median
Price / Sales (TTM)	B	1.66	2.67
Price / Sales (FWD)	B-	2.08	2.71
Price / Book (TTM)	A-	1.04	2.96
Price / Book (FWD)	A	1.08	3.72
Price / Cash Flow (TTM)	A	6.84	19.63
Price / Cash Flow (FWD)	B+	12.34	17.80
Dividend Yield (TTM)	A+	5.72%	1.58%

Figure 18: *Intel valuation metrics compared to sector peers (Source: Seeking Alpha)*

Investors have become very pessimistic about INTC's prospects and are shedding its stock like there is no tomorrow – so much so that the company has become highly undervalued. It is a colossal mistake that the herd is making, given that INTC's prospects will improve from H2 2023. INTC is available almost at its book value (TTM Price/Book ratio is a mere 1.04). Other stocks in the same league are available at a TTM Price/Book ratio of 2.96. Aside from the fact that the stock is currently cheaply available – INTC's TTM dividend yield is a hefty 5.72% – which makes it very attractive even to income investors.

The implications are clear – old investors have dumped INTC and new investors are unwilling to consider its solid business prospects.

Summing Up

INTC's robust balance sheet, improving prospects from H2 2023, an exciting 2024 to look forward to, and its current undervalued price should not be ignored by prudent long-term growth and income investors.

Plus, given the unavoidable proliferation of AI in the future, we believe that INTC makes for a solid long-term investment for both growth and income investors at its current price at the time of printing (around $30).

Meta Platforms: Social Media Weds Artificial Intelligence

META has been slipping and sliding since September 2021. By October 2022, it had fallen by as much as 74% but has retraced quite a bit. Though the stock has recovered somewhat, it is still available at a discount of about 48% from its September 2021 highs.

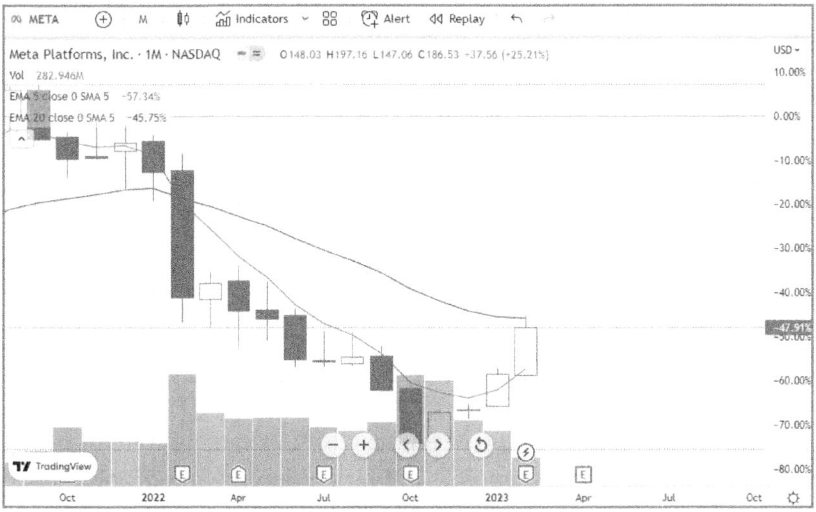

Figure 19: *Meta price chart vs. all time high between October 2022 and February 2023 Intel (Source: TradingView)*

A variety of factors caused the META fall. To begin with, in 2021, Apple's privacy policies hit its ad revenues, because of which the earnings dropped. META's Reels feature did not generate the expected advertising revenue. Additionally, the number of active users decreased, and the Fed started hiking interest rates. But these negatives are now behind us.

META is now focused on exploiting the double muscle of AI (in the medium term) and the Metaverse (in the long term) to take itself to the next level. We believe that META (currently at about $187) has solid long-term potential, and here are our reasons why.

A. New Developments At META

1. The latest data reveals that more than 3.7 billion people use META's apps (FaceBook, Instagram, WhatsApp) every month, with more than 2 billion people using FaceBook daily. These are the highest numbers the company has ever witnessed.

2. The company continues to optimize its operations. In 2022, it laid off people, stopped working on unproductive projects, and restructured its teams. In 2023, the company intends to focus on increasing efficiencies by spending on essential infrastructure, thereby saving on CapEx. Other restructuring moves include flattening its organizational structure to make decision-making quicker and equipping its engineers with AI tools to increase productivity.

3. META is also focused on improving its financial performance from 2023 onwards by investing aggressively in technologies likely to shape the future. The company foresees AI and the Metaverse as the two technology waves that will shape our future. So, Facebook and Instagram are being reorganized from delivering content based on people/accounts that users follow to content served by META's AI systems. In Q4 2022, META's advertisers witnessed an increase of 20% in conversions, year over year, and that too at a lower cost per acquisition.

4. Reels, which play across Instagram and Facebook, are growing in popularity. Users have doubled in the last 12 months, while the usage of its resharing component has doubled in the previous 6 months. META is currently improving Reels' monetization efficiency (revenue/minute). Though the current monetization of Reels' is below that of the other feeds on Facebook and Instagram,

the company believes that Reels increases engagement levels. META expects to improve Reels' monetization efficiency this year.

5. META's Business Messaging (on WhatsApp) vertical is the third pillar of its business after Facebook and Instagram. Recently, Air France started using WhatsApp to share boarding passes/ information across 22 countries and in four languages. META also intends to begin milking this revenue source from 2023 onwards.

6. The company's R&D department is focused on building generative AI, which can extend across many applications. The company continues its Metaverse quest, which it believes has solid long-term potential. The company shipped its Quest Pro VR Headset in December 2022, which is believed to set the standard for the Metaverse. Many VR applications are being created that Quest Pro can access – for example, Nanome for 3D modeling, Arkio for architects, and more. Technology is diversifying and increasing; it is a matter of time before the Metaverse lands upon us. When it does, META will be right at the forefront to cash in on it.

B. META's Financials

	TTM	Dec 2022	Dec 2021	Dec 2020	Dec 2019
Revenues					
Revenues	116,609.0	116,609.0	117,929.0	85,965.0	70,697.0
Other Revenues	-	-	-	-	-
Total Revenues	**116,609.0**	**116,609.0**	**117,929.0**	**85,965.0**	**70,697.0**
Cost Of Revenues	23,754.0	23,754.0	22,649.0	16,692.0	12,770.0
Gross Profit	**92,855.0**	**92,855.0**	**95,280.0**	**69,273.0**	**57,927.0**
Operating Expenses & Income					
Selling General & Admin Expenses	25,681.0	25,681.0	23,872.0	18,155.0	15,341.0
R&D Expenses	33,619.0	33,619.0	24,655.0	18,447.0	13,600.0
Total Operating Expenses	59,300.0	59,300.0	48,527.0	36,602.0	28,941.0
Operating Income	**33,555.0**	**33,555.0**	**46,753.0**	**32,671.0**	**28,986.0**

Figure 20: *Meta Income Statement for the previous 4 years (Source: Seeking Alpha)*

It is evident that META's profits have started growing again. The company revenues of $32 billion in Q4 2022 are up about 17% quarter over quarter, and operating income of $10.60 billion is up 74% quarter over quarter. These numbers have leapfrogged because META's focus on AI and the Metaverse has started paying off.

META Profitability Grade A+			
	Sector Relative Grade	META	Sector Median
Gross Profit Margin (TTM)	A	79.63%	49.63%
EBIT Margin (TTM)	A+	28.78%	9.32%
EBITDA Margin (TTM)	A	36.22%	18.78%
Net Income Margin (TTM)	A	19.90%	3.34%
Levered FCF Margin (TTM)	B+	13.38%	8.88%
Return on Common Equity (TTM)	A-	18.52%	3.62%
Return on Total Capital (TTM)	A+	14.38%	3.54%
Return on Total Assets (TTM)	A+	12.49%	1.68%
CAPEX / Sales (TTM)	A+	26.95%	3.90%
Asset Turnover Ratio (TTM)	B	0.66x	0.47x
Cash From Operations (TTM)	A+	50.48B	210.42M
Net Income Per Employee (TTM)	A+	268.26K	10.99K

Figure 21: *Meta profitability metrics vs. sector peers (Source: Seeking Alpha)*

META's profitability ratios are astounding. A net income margin of 20% (sector median: 3.34%), a 12.5% return on total assets (sector median: 2%), and a net income per employee of $286K (sector median: $10.99K) provide enough evidence that the company is hugely profitable and very efficiently managed. Now throw in the improving prospects, AI, and the Metaverse, and you can see the bull case in full swing.

In a balance sheet of $185 billion, META has $41 billion in cash and short-term investments (22% of the company's balance sheet). Net property, plant & equipment make up about 50% of its balance sheet, while the long-term debt works out to just 5.5% of its balance sheet.

The company has recently announced a massive buyback of $40 billion worth of its stock, and we believe it has done so because it feels its stock is undervalued. We agree.

Summing Up

META has everything going for it:

1. A robust balance sheet
2. Growing profitability
3. Plenty of liquidity
4. Very little long-term debt
5. A shareholder-friendly management
6. Fascinating prospects (AI, Metaverse)
7. A beaten-down stock price

You name it; META's got it. There is just one slight hiccup: The Fed may raise rates beyond 5%, which might dampen bulls in the short term. However, if you are a serious long-term investor, META is a coffee can stock to latch on to. It is a one-of-a-kind stock that boosts social media with AI and makes the virtual world feel real with its devices.

Microsoft: Pure AI Power

Microsoft (MSFT) is steadily on its way to becoming an AI powerhouse. Though the Fed's interest rate hikes and recessionary signs have made its customers optimize their digital spending. Microsoft is preparing for the next revolution in computing by converting the world's most sophisticated AI models into a unified computing platform.

MSFT's sales data prove beyond doubt that AI is the sector to thrive in – in Q2 2022-23 (the company's fiscal year ends on June 30), Microsoft Cloud's revenues crossed $27 billion, registering a hefty 29% increase quarter on quarter. There was plenty more action which you will read about below.

Our team of researchers believes that MSFT has the makings of a solid long-term growth story and here are the reasons why.

A. MSFT's Focus on AI

1. Big companies have already moved millions of calls to MSFT's Azure. As of Q2 2023, enterprises ran twice the number of calls on Azure than they did 2 years ago. Despite the enormous volume increase, MSFT believes that these are early days and the long-term opportunity has yet to mature. The transition to AI is picking up speed as well – For example, the MSFT cloud platform backed by its AI tools helped AIA, the insurance company, save 20% of its costs. Azure Arc, one of Microsoft's hybrid computing platforms, has over 12,000 customers, up from 6,000 customers a year back.
2. The Microsoft Intelligent Data Platform helps customers integrate data at a lower cost and derive superior real-time results using powerful AI tools. Currently, MSFT has 26 million global customers using this platform.
3. The company believes it has the most potent AI supercomputing infrastructure (Azure AI Services) in the cloud. Millions of its customers and partners use this infrastructure to develop cutting-edge tools and services, one of them being ChatGPT. In the third week of January 2023, MSFT opened its Azure OpenAI service, and enterprises such as Al Jazeera and KPMG signed up for it. MSFT has also become OpenAI's exclusive cloud partner. The transition to AI is happening so rapidly that Azure Machine Learning's revenue has increased by over 100% for 5 quarters in a row!

4. The company's Power Platform, which equips enterprises with automation, virtual agents, and business intelligence, which help them simplify repetitive tasks, currently leads the competition in robotic process automation. It has over 45,000 customers – up 50% year over year.

5. MSFT's solutions for the retail industry helped Zabka, a Poland-based retailer, build the largest chain of independent stores in the EU. The company has partnered with the London Stock Exchange Group for financial data analytics services. In healthcare, MSFT has become the partner of choice for any company wanting to harness the power of AI to improve patients' interactions with their doctors.

6. MSFT's security business exceeded $20 billion in revenue, mainly because it is the only company that can provide end-to-end tools covering identity, compliance, device management, cloud security, and privacy.

7. It is not just AI that MSFT is trying to cash in on – the company has a significant presence in just about any business you can think of – from careers (LinkedIn) to office tools to team building, to collaboration tools and even gaming!

8. MSFT is about to revolutionize its Bing search engine by incorporating ChatGPT. ChatGPT is a conversational AI search bot that is creating waves worldwide. It has over 100 million users and is the fastest-growing app in the world. This could help Bing finally make a dent in Google's search monopoly.

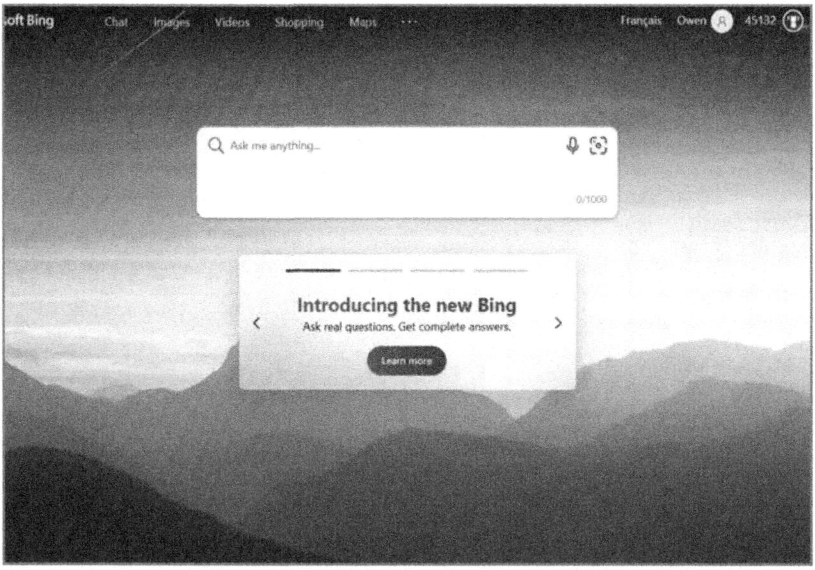

Figure 22: *Microsoft Bing with ChatGPT integration (Source: Microsoft)*

B. MSFT's Stunning Profitability Ratios

MSFT Profitability Grade A+

	Sector Relative Grade	MSFT	Sector Median
Gross Profit Margin (TTM)	B+	68.16%	49.19%
EBIT Margin (TTM)	A+	40.97%	5.88%
EBITDA Margin (TTM)	A+	47.99%	11.22%
Net Income Margin (TTM)	A+	33.05%	2.92%
Levered FCF Margin (TTM)	A-	21.86%	6.73%
Return on Common Equity (TTM)	A+	39.31%	4.87%
Return on Total Capital (TTM)	A+	20.84%	3.21%
Return on Total Assets (TTM)	A+	18.50%	1.54%
CAPEX / Sales (TTM)	A	12.14%	2.41%
Asset Turnover Ratio (TTM)	C+	0.58x	0.61x
Cash From Operations (TTM)	A+	84.39B	56.01M
Net Income Per Employee (TTM)	A+	305.20K	4,459.72

Figure 23: *Microsoft profitability metrics vs. sector peers (Source: Seeking Alpha)*

MSFT's profitability ratios are simply the best in the industry. An 20.84% return on total capital (sector median: 3.21%), a net income margin of 33.05% (sector median: 2.92%), and a net income of $305.20K per employee (sector median: $4.46K) say it all.

Think about it for a minute and visualize that MSFT now leads the AI-transitioning movement, and all that you may see is growing revenues, profits, dividends, and buybacks.

C. MSFT's Robust Balance Sheet

Between 2018 and TTM 2023, MSFT's net fixed assets (property, plant & equipment) have jumped by a whopping 267% (from $36 billion to $ 96 billion). Goodwill and intangible assets have jumped by almost 100% in the same period. All these investments in hard assets, R&D, and acquisitions have started to pay off today. Azure, data analytics, Data Intelligence, and many more MSFT platforms that were in the making have started generating big-time money, which is reflected in the company's profitability ratios.

In a balance sheet of $364.50 billion, MSFT owns cash and short-term investments worth $99.5 billion (about 27% of the total balance sheet), which gives it sufficient dry powder to take on the competition and acquire companies that can increase its competitiveness.

Summing Up

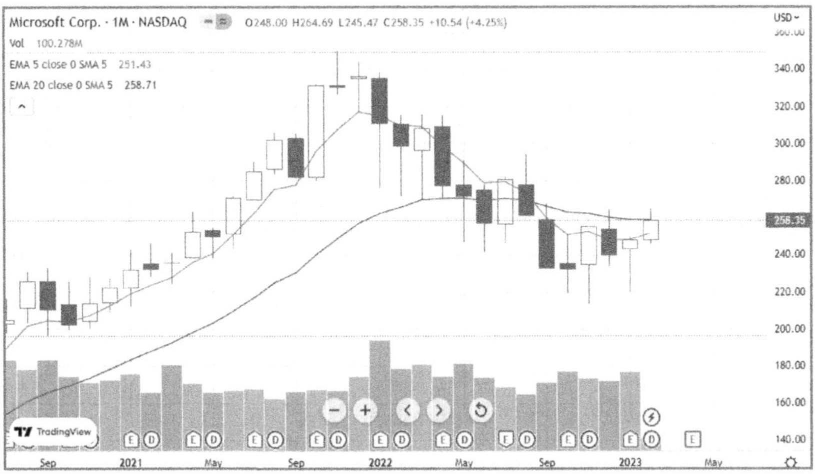

Figure 24: *Microsoft price chart between September 2021 and February 2023 (Source: TradingView)*

MSFT's monthly charts show that the stock has fallen from about $350 to about $270 at the time of writing. The fall began after the Russia-Ukraine war and interest rate hikes, events that hit technology stocks the hardest. MSFT is hovering around its 20-month average, and any breakout from these levels can imply that the game is on and the investors have started chasing the stock.

That was what the technical charts show – aside from that, the current financials and the prospects for the company, especially its AI businesses, seem too outstanding to ignore.

Therefore, despite a high Forward Price/Earnings ratio of 28.5, we are incredibly bullish on MSFT as a solid pick for serious long-term investors. Don't miss this AI juggernaut – you may regret it.

Nvidia: The Headwinds Are Now A Breeze

NVIDIA Corporation (NVDA) has survived a very volatile 2022–23. The stock plunged to a low of $108 in 2022 but has recovered substantially and closed at about $233 as of February 24, 2023. If you take a longer view of the stock, it has delivered solid 279% gains in the last 5 years and a massive 7,228% gain over the previous 10 years.

The stock suffered in 2022 because of the Fed's hawkish policies, Chinese lockdowns due to COVID-19, and the general recessionary trends caused by the Russia–Ukraine war.

We believe that the Fed rate may peak at 5.25%, or, in the worst case, at 5.5%, and then all the recent layoffs in the tech and financial sectors will start taking their toll on the economic data – at this time, the Fed may pause hiking the rates and start rolling them back. Though we cannot time the Fed's moves, we believe that the Fed may begin rolling back the interest rates by August–September 2023.

By this time, many AI apps will start changing our virtual and, perhaps, real lives. And when the time comes to buy high-quality AI stocks like NVDA, the stock prices may already be touching sky-high levels.

Now, here is why we consider NVDA to be a solid portfolio pick for serious long-term investors:

The Latest Developments at NVDA

1. The company's management believes that the demand for GPUs and AI infrastructure remains strong despite the macroeconomic uncertainty. However, networking demand (CPU infrastructure) was soft mainly because of lower demand from China (COVID-19 lockdown, which was recently lifted).

2. Data Centers are growing rapidly and Cloud Service Providers (CSP) have contributed 40% to NVDA's TTM revenues.

3. NVDA's H100 chip, which is 9 times faster than its A100 chip, saw a massive increase in demand. That is because the H100, which is 30 times faster than competitors' chips, helps customers work on transformer-based large language models (AI apps like ChatGPT, Google Bard, and many more to come). The H100 and NVDA's Infiniband range of products, helps its users work on large language models with more than 100 billion parameters.

4. NVDA is already one-up over the competition in AI. The manufacturers and providers of supercomputers, algorithms and generative AI developers trust its products and services. In Q4 2022, NVDA partnered with Deutsche Bank to use AI and machine learning in the financial services sector. The partnership aims to develop applications that include virtual customer service agents, fraud detection, and automation of bank processes.

5. The company is almost ready to launch NeMo and BioNeMo, which are large language model services.

6. NVDA also offers the NVIDIA DGX Cloud, wherein customers can deploy its AI cloud services by using its supercomputer, acceleration library software, or pre-trained AI model layers.

7. Needless to add, NVDA's chips and GPUs are the leaders in gaming systems. In February 2023, NVDA entered into a 10-year partnership with Microsoft to bring GeForce NOW to Xbox PC games.

8. NVDA's CEO believes that the current AI usage is just the inflection point and that the company is poised to achieve much more significant milestones in the future.

As AI changes how we experience the Internet and develop content or apps, NVDA is perched right up there to take a nice chunk of AI business that can be imagined but not foreseen. The AI story has just begun for NVDA.

NVDA's Robust Financials

Cash Flow Statement (Quarterly)

Financials in millions USD. Fiscal year is February - January.

Quarter Ended	2023-01-29	2022-10-30	2022-07-31	2022-05-01	2022-01-30
Net Income	**1,414**	**680**	**656**	**1,618**	**3,003**
Depreciation & Amortization	426	406	378	334	309
Share-Based Compensation	738	745	648	578	551
Other Operating Activities	-330	-1,439	-412	-799	-830
Operating Cash Flow	**2,248**	**392**	**1,270**	**1,731**	**3,033**
Operating Cash Flow Growth	-25.88%	-74.19%	-52.65%	-7.63%	46.73%
Capital Expenditures	-509	-530	-433	-361	-273
Acquisitions	0	0	-13	-36	-60
Change in Investments	506	3,678	2,064	3,009	-1,253
Other Investing Activities	-	-	-	-	-
Investing Cash Flow	**-3**	**3,148**	**1,618**	**2,612**	**-1,586**
Dividends Paid	-98	-100	-100	-100	-101
Share Issuance / Repurchase	-1,207	-3,341	-3,344	-1,792	4
Debt Issued / Paid	-4	-18	-14	-22	-21
Other Financing Activities	-347	-294	-304	-532	-627
Financing Cash Flow	**-1,656**	**-3,753**	**-3,762**	**-2,446**	**-745**
Net Cash Flow	**589**	**-213**	**-874**	**1,897**	**702**
Free Cash Flow	1,739	-138	837	1,370	2,760

Figure 25: *Nvidia Cash Flow Statement for the previous 5 quarters (Source: stockanalysis.com)*

In Q4 2022, NVDA generated $2.2 billion in operating cash against $392 million in Q3 2022. The increase occurred because of efficient working capital management. In a balance sheet of $41 billion, NVDA's cash and short-term investments have swelled to a whopping $13 billion, or 32% of the balance sheet.

This war chest, leadership status, and quality AI products give NVDA an unbeatable lead.

NVDA Profitability Grade A+

	Sector Relative Grade	NVDA	Sector Median
Gross Profit Margin (TTM)	B-	56.93%	49.19%
EBIT Margin (TTM)	A	20.68%	5.88%
EBITDA Margin (TTM)	A-	26.40%	11.22%
Net Income Margin (TTM)	A	16.19%	2.92%
Levered FCF Margin (TTM)	B+	16.80%	6.73%
Return on Common Equity (TTM)	A-	17.93%	4.87%
Return on Total Capital (TTM)	A-	9.61%	3.21%
Return on Total Assets (TTM)	A	10.61%	1.54%
CAPEX / Sales (TTM)	A-	6.80%	2.41%
Asset Turnover Ratio (TTM)	C+	0.63x	0.61x
Cash From Operations (TTM)	A+	5.64B	56.01M
Net Income Per Employee (TTM)	A+	166.74K	4,459.72

Figure 26: *Nvidia profitability metrics vs. sector peers (Source: Seeking Alpha)*

It is a no-brainer that NVDA has a solid and winnable lead over its competitors any way you look at it. Technology, AI, balance sheet, profitability, operating efficiency, R&D, products – you name it, NVDA has it all. This is why the company reports a superior net income margin of 16.19% (sector median: 2.92%), levered FCF margin of 16.80% (sector median: 6.73%), and a net income of $194.37K per employee (sector median: $4.46K).

We believe that as AI proliferates, NVDA's profits, cash balance and equivalents, dividends, buybacks, and share price will increase and the stock will stand out as an outperformer in the long run.

Summing Up

Nvidia is perhaps the most direct bet on the AI revolution you can make. That being said, there are near-term valuation concerns. It's difficult to justify paying 150x earnings at the best times, let alone for a company forecasting moderate revenue and earnings growth in the next 18 months.

Still, we are bullish on NVDA as a long-term coffee-can stock. We also believe it will maintain its industry leadership status in the coming years. If you don't have a position yet, it's essential to be patient and avoid chasing the stock at any price.

Perion Network: In A New Orbit Now

Suddenly and immediately after the launch of ChatGPT, Perion Network (PERI) shot into the major league of the digital advertising world. For those who are not aware, in November 2020, PERI's technology division (CodeFuel) renewed its partnership with Microsoft (MSFT) for 4 years. This partnership collaborates on growing search advertising business and creating an immersive experience across all devices.

Now, MSFT is all set to launch ChatGPT, a transformative AI chatbot, in its new Bing search engine, which will undoubtedly change the face of search and digital advertising. It will change how advertisers interact with their audience and potentially create new advertising avenues. As of print, MSFT has a 3% share in the global search market, and the new Bing will help it increase its share. We believe that MSFT's share in the worldwide search market will double, at the very least. Know that a 1% global search market equals about $2 billion worth of advertising revenue, and every percentage gain for Bing will generate solid additional revenues for PERI. Imagine what will happen at PERI if Bing captures a 10% share of the global search market!!

We believe that ChatGPT has massively increased PERI's long-term investment quotient.

With that said, here are a few other factors that increase PERI's attractiveness:

Other Developments at PERI

PERI has an AI engine (called ENGINE AI) that suggests optimized solutions for brands, agencies, and publishers. The engine balances the demand and supply of advertisers and publishers, understands the context, and offers optimized and productive solutions in real time after processing billions of requests daily.

In Q4 2022, the company witnessed a surge in demand for live CTV advertising (advertisements that appear within live streaming content). The management expects that the trend will only get bullish from here on. In 2022, PERI's video platform registered a solid growth of 129%, year over year, and formed 43% of its display advertising revenue.

A thumb rule in the IT industry says that a software company's combined revenue growth rate and profit margin should equal or exceed 40% - this is known as "The Rule of 40" In Q4 2022, PERI registered a 54% growth based on the abovementioned parameter.

PERI's suite of AI products includes SORT, a cookie-less solution which uses machine learning to analyze millions of data combinations to create target groups. This solution is picking up traction. In Q4 2022, SORT generated $26 million, an 82% increase quarter over quarter. The SORT revenues formed 21% of PERI's advertising revenue, and the number of customers using SORT increased by 36%, quarter over quarter.

PERI's search advertising increases the number of publishers and monetized searchers transferred to Microsoft Bing. The company registered an average of 22 million daily searches in Q4 2022, up 26% year over year. In Q1 2023, the company recorded an average of 25 million daily searches. Now imagine what will happen to these numbers when ChatGPT is built into the new Bing.

Income Statement (Annual)

Financials in millions USD. Fiscal year is January - December.

Year	2022	2021	2020	2019
Revenue	**640.26**	**478.5**	**328.06**	**261.45**
Revenue Growth (YoY)	33.81%	45.86%	25.48%	3.40%
Cost of Revenue	403.01	313.22	220.1	161.41
Gross Profit	**237.25**	**165.28**	**107.96**	**100.04**
Selling, General & Admin	79.83	74.14	54.9	49.74
Research & Development	34.42	35.35	30.88	22.59
Other Operating Expenses	13.84	9.9	9.92	9.71
Operating Expenses	128.09	119.39	95.71	82.03
Operating Income	**109.16**	**45.9**	**12.25**	**18.01**
Interest Expense / Income	-4.5	0.58	2.64	3.47
Other Expense / Income	-	-	-	-
Pretax Income	**113.66**	**45.32**	**9.62**	**14.54**
Income Tax	14.44	6.61	-0.61	1.65
Net Income	**99.23**	**38.71**	**10.23**	**12.89**

PERI's Financials

Figure 27: *Perion Network Income Statement for the previous 4 years (Source: stockanalysis.com)*

PERI's income and operating profits are not just growing – they are zooming! The company reported revenues of $210 million and an operating income of $41 million in Q4 2022. The numbers represented an increase of 32% in sales and 39% in operating income quarter over quarter. The number of searchers is increasing, PERI's AI is getting more cutting-edge, and ChatGPT is about to be built into Bing. So, potential investors can expect a substantial jump in revenues, operating income, and net income in 2023 and beyond.

Cash Flow Statement (Annual)

Financials in millions USD. Fiscal year is January - December.

Year	2022	2021	2020	2019
Net Income	**99.23**	**38.71**	**10.23**	**12.89**
Depreciation & Amortization	13.84	9.9	9.92	9.71
Share-Based Compensation	11.57	6.99	4.45	2.29
Other Operating Activities	-2.51	15.52	-2.44	19.84
Operating Cash Flow	**122.12**	**71.11**	**22.16**	**44.74**
Operating Cash Flow Growth	71.74%	220.89%	-50.47%	36.40%
Capital Expenditures	-1.05	-0.53	-0.45	-0.72
Acquisitions	-9.57	-38.44	-19	-1.2
Change in Investments	-36.2	-204.5	10.53	-19.23
Other Investing Activities	-	-	-	-
Investing Cash Flow	**-46.82**	**-243.47**	**-8.92**	**-21.15**
Dividends Paid	0	0	0	0
Share Issuance / Repurchase	5.83	237.39	4.29	1.23
Debt Issued / Paid	0	-8.33	-8.33	-24.18
Other Financing Activities	-9.09	-	-	-1.81
Financing Cash Flow	**-3.26**	**229.05**	**-4.05**	**-24.77**
Net Cash Flow	**71.99**	**56.66**	**9.27**	**-1.2**
Free Cash Flow	121.07	70.57	21.71	44.02

Figure 28: *Perion Network Cash Flow Statement for the previous 4 years (Source: stockanalysis.com)*

PERI generates positive operating cash flows consistently – a healthy sign. In Q4 2022, the company generated $38 million in operating cash, up 10% quarter over quarter and 33% year over year. As reasoned above, the company's profits are set to rise, and we believe that its operating cash flows are also set to grow at a healthy rate.

PERI's profitability ratios are already outstanding. A solid net income margin of 15.50% (sector median: 3.25%), a healthy return on total assets of 11.40% (sector median: 1.77%), and a robust net income per employee of $249K (sector median: $11.73K) suggest that the company is not just very profitable, but it is very efficiently managed. Now imagine the serious bump-ups that PERI's profitability will receive after ChatGPT is integrated into Bing.

In a balance sheet of $870 million, PERI has:

(a) $430 million in cash and short-term investments. In other words, about 49% of PERI's total assets are very liquid. This gives the company sufficient resources to intensify its R&D processes after Chat GPT is built into Bing. At that time, digital advertising as we know it will change and companies like PERI need to be ready for it.

(b) PERI has ZERO long-term debt. That is a considerable advantage in a business environment where interest rates are being raised almost every two months.

Summing Up

We are convinced that PERI has an extremely bright future and that its journey has just begun. AI is recently being introduced in search engines – and this is just the beginning. What would happen if AI gets into multimedia-mode? This includes, for example, the conversion of text into music or videos, writing songs and creating videos on the fly, and more. We believe such innovations will change the face of the Internet as we know it.

We believe that the AI action has just about started and well-managed companies like PERI will witness a massive increase in business and R&D activities. Plus, the company still trades at a very reasonable multiple (17x earnings). Therefore, we are very bullish on PERI as a medium-to-long-term portfolio stock.

What about X/Y/Z stock?!

Whenever we make lists like these, we get many questions from readers asking why we didn't include certain other companies. Even with this book, our advanced preview readers questioned why companies like Apple, Taiwan Semiconductor and ASML weren't included in this list.

The first thing to address is that just because these companies didn't make the final cut doesn't mean there is anything inherently wrong with them or that they don't have potential. It's simply a matter of brevity. The AI revolution will bring up many winners, including some not included in this book. Our criteria was 7 companies that we believe are firmly positioned to benefit from the growing AI industry.

That being said, we always welcome healthy discussion and feedback, and that's precisely what we do inside our free community called **High Conviction Investors**. You can join us there and let us know your stocks that will be big winners in the coming years.

It's completely free, and you also get access to our bonus resources and training inside as well.

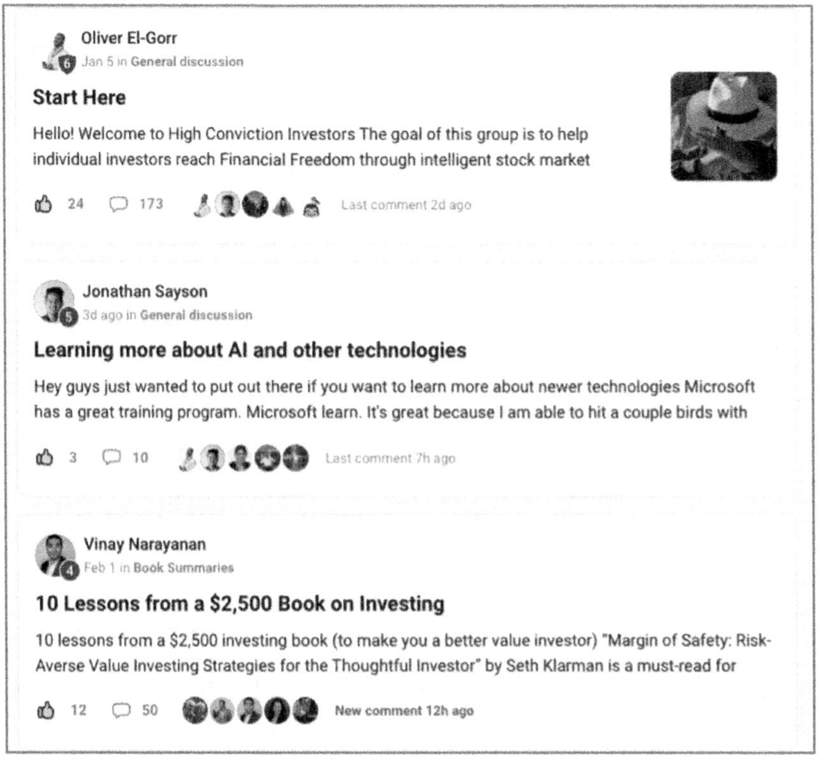

Join us by going to freemanpublications.com/community

Chapter 9

4 AI STOCKS TO AVOID

Saying that a stock's investable value is high just because the company has an AI component is entirely incorrect. While it's true that AI has the potential to transform our lives in ways we couldn't have predicted a few years ago, assuming that every AI-focused company is a good investment is a big mistake.

It is difficult for every company or start-up in the AI sector to succeed, mainly because the competitors are giants (GOOG, MSFT, AAPL, NVDA, to name a few), and the tech obsolescence factor is very high.

So, while some solidly investable AI stocks are out there, we have dug deep and mined 4 AI companies that are burning cash and depreciating investor wealth. We believe that these companies should be avoided. Here is the list:

Big Bear.ai Holdings (BBAI)

BBAI, which provides AI and machine learning solutions to governments, healthcare, and manufacturing segments, has destroyed the wealth of its loyal shareholders. Since 2018 the stock has fallen by about 65%, with a 34% fall occurring in the last 12 months. In 2023, the stock has zoomed from about $0.56 to $3.42 (as of February 23, 2023), a move that was cashed in on by speculators and operators but not by genuine investors.

BBAI reported a lower negative operating loss of $8.2 million and a lower net loss of $16.10 million in Q3 2022, quarter over quarter. It also reported a lower net cash burn of $7.9 million in the same quarter.

BBAI's balance sheet too seems below par:

Financials in millions USD. Fiscal year is January - December.

Quarter Ended	2022-09-30	2022-06-30	2022-03-31	2021-12-31
Cash & Equivalents	21.96	29.83	59.98	169.92
Cash & Cash Equivalents	**21.96**	**29.83**	**59.98**	**169.92**
Cash Growth	-	232.17%	-	1651.04%
Receivables	31.65	28.55	26.62	28.61
Other Current Assets	6.41	9.35	9.54	7.66
Total Current Assets	**60.01**	**67.72**	**96.14**	**206.18**
Property, Plant & Equipment	1.53	1.43	1.34	1.08
Goodwill and Intangibles	154.68	156.62	173.61	175.28
Other Long-Term Assets	0.69	0.73	0.74	0.78
Total Long-Term Assets	**156.9**	**158.78**	**175.69**	**177.14**
Total Assets	**216.91**	**226.5**	**271.83**	**383.32**
Accounts Payable	7.43	6.35	6.63	5.48
Deferred Revenue	4.76	3.71	2.79	4.21
Current Debt	0.77	1.92	3.07	4.23
Other Current Liabilities	19.78	16.86	17.67	56.1
Total Current Liabilities	**32.74**	**28.85**	**30.16**	**70.02**
Long-Term Debt	191.83	191.34	190.85	190.36
Other Long-Term Liabilities	0.44	0.53	0.77	0.57
Total Long-Term Liabilities	**192.27**	**191.87**	**191.62**	**190.94**

Figure 29: *Big Bear AI Balance Sheet for the previous 4 quarters (Source: stockanalysis.com)*

In a balance sheet of $217 million, BBAI owns intangible assets worth $155 million (71% of the total balance sheet). The company's cash and equivalents are just $22 million, and if the company continues to burn cash as it did in Q3 2022, its cash balances will turn negative in the space of three quarters. BBAI's long-term debt is a whopping $192 million, or 88% of its balance sheet, and its common equity has been almost wiped off by its accumulated losses.

ContextLogic (WISH)

WISH, a global mobile e-commerce marketplace, was listed in late 2020. Since then, WISH has erased a whopping 96.44% of its shareholders' wealth. It is now a penny stock, going at $0.72, and it continues to burn cash quarter over quarter. Here is a quick take on why this stock should be avoided even though it is deploying AI to enhance its customer experience, increase eyeballs, and retain buyers:

1. WISH's CEO has stated in the company's Q4 2022 earnings call that revenues and ad spending took a hit as consumers cut down their discretionary product spending because of high-interest rates. He added: "there's still much more work ahead to do to put us back on the path to profitability and growth." Well, we believe that "much work to do" could take several years that could exhaust investor tenacity.

Balance Sheet (Annual)

Financials in millions USD. Fiscal year is January - December.

Year	2022	2021	2020
Cash & Equivalents	1,050	1,706	2,130
Short-Term Investments	228	693	462
Cash & Cash Equivalents	**1,278**	**2,399**	**2,592**
Cash Growth	-46.73%	-7.45%	162.61%
Receivables	272	226	110
Inventory	90	69	52
Other Current Assets	293	318	292
Total Current Assets	**1,933**	**3,012**	**3,046**
Accounts Payable	1,204	1,166	1,157
Deferred Revenue	0	0	0
Other Current Liabilities	868	1,051	1,009
Total Current Liabilities	**2,072**	**2,217**	**2,166**
Long-Term Debt	4,030	3,944	3,529
Other Long-Term Liabilities	28	28	67
Total Long-Term Liabilities	**4,058**	**3,972**	**3,596**
Total Liabilities	**6,130**	**6,189**	**5,762**
Total Debt	**4,030**	**3,944**	**3,529**

Figure 30: *Wish Balance Sheet for the previous 3 years (Source: stockanalysis.com)*

2. WISH's balance sheet looks like a disaster in the making. Its cash has dramatically reduced from $2.4B billion as of December 2021 to $1.2B as of December 2022. The reduction is because of losses. In Q4 2022, marketplace revenue was down 72% year over year, and the net loss reported formed 89% of the quarterly revenue. Operating cash flows were a negative $109 million on revenues of $123 million in Q4 2022. Any which you look at WISH's financials, WISH looks like an AI stock to stay away from.

Robinhood Markets (HOOD)

HOOD, a commission-free trading app, and a meme stock has destroyed about 82% of its loyal shareholder's wealth since its listing in 2021. It had its day in the sun when the COVID-19 lockdowns in 2020–21 forced the people to stay indoors and, well, spend some time trading the markets, which were booming like there was no tomorrow. All that has changed since the Fed started hiking interest rates and lockdowns were lifted. It is time now to get down to brass tacks, and HOOD's brass tacks do not look so good.

For starters, HOOD has too much competition (Stash, ETrade, WeBull, and others, with Stash leading the pack). Secondly, for HOOD to report the kind of revenues it did in 2021, the market has to start melting up like it did when COVID-19 forced the Fed to slash interest rates.

In Q4 2021, HOOD clocked brokerage revenues of $264 million, and in Q4 2022 revenues fell to $186 million. Though HOOD keeps working on its AI to help investors pick the best stocks, the competition has caught up and HOOD has its work cut out. In 2020, the company generated operating cash flows of $1.9 billion, while it reported negative operating cash flows of $852 million in 2022.

AI or no AI, it will be a long, hard grind for HOOD going forward and we urge you to stay away from it.

Peleton Interactive (PTON)

Exercise equipment maker Peleton Interactive (PTON) uses AI to mix its customers' data with open-source data, then recommends customized exercises per their individual needs and tracks their progress. The company's AI-supported computer vision recognizes customer activity and makes working out an interactive process. We wish the company had created something as potent as this for their shareholders.

In the last 12 months, PTON has destroyed about 56% of its shareholder wealth and continues to burn cash.

	Dec 2022	Sep 2022	Jun 2022	Mar 2022
Revenues				
Revenues	792.7	616.5	678.7	964.3
Other Revenues	-	-	(0.1)	-
Total Revenues	**792.7**	**616.5**	**678.6**	**964.3**
Cost Of Revenues	553.9	399.3	708.5	780.1
Gross Profit	**238.8**	**217.2**	**(29.9)**	**184.2**
Operating Expenses & Income				
Selling General & Admin Expenses	390.4	326.5	359.1	432.8
R&D Expenses	80.0	88.1	84.9	77.1
Total Operating Expenses	470.4	414.6	444.0	509.9
Operating Income	**(231.6)**	**(197.4)**	**(473.9)**	**(325.7)**

Figure 31: *Peloton Income Statement for the previous 4 quarters (Source: stockanalysis.com)*

In Q4 2022, PTON reported revenues of $793 million compared to $1.1 billion in Q4 2021 – a decline of 31% year over year. However, the company did report a lower net operating loss of $232 million in Q4 2022, but that was only because it slashed its operating expenses (see the image above). Discretionary spending is reducing with the Fed rate hikes hitting businesses and disposable incomes hard. As the Fed is likely to start lowering rates only after inflation is brought under control, it does seem that companies like PTON will have no option but to tackle falling sales by slashing costs. But that's not an investment story investors should chase.

Moreover, more than 50% of PTON's balance sheet of $3.3 billion is represented by long-term debt and the company's paid-in capital of $4.4 billion has been completely wiped out by its accumulated losses.

We believe that PTON is another self-touted AI stock to avoid.

KEY TAKEAWAYS

- ◇ AI is not a guarantee of success - Just because a company claims to be involved in the AI sector or has an AI element to its business model... does not automatically make it a good investment. Many businesses in this industry face intense competition and rapid rates of technological obsolescence.
- ◇ Avoid companies that burn cash without showing signs of long-term profitability including Big Bear.ai Holdings (BBAI), ContextLogic (WISH), Robinhood Markets (HOOD), and Peleton Interactive (PTON).
- ◇ When investing in AI companies, it is crucial to examine the company's financial health, such as its balance sheet, cash burn rate, and debt levels, as well as the competitive landscape it operates in before buying the stock

Chapter 10

CAN AI HELP YOU BEAT THE STOCK MARKET?

The market is not static, it's dynamic; things change. Therefore I think there's room for new inefficiencies to materialize. I think it's never going to be that all inefficiencies are out with nothing new to discover.

- Jim Simons.

A computer science degree with four decades of experience in the fields of AI, alternative computing, image processing, and cyber security makes an unlikely profile for the head of an investment firm. However, Jeff Glickman, owner of several technology patents, took up the challenge to create a self-learning computer system that could beat a human investor in the stock market. In 2020, he claimed to have achieved a success rate of 60% - incredible by all counts, considering that even a 51% success rate would give an investor a tremendous edge in the market. His success did not materialize in one day or even a year.

It was around 2000 when Glickman started toying with the idea of predicting stock price movement based on the Brownian motion of objects suspended in a liquid. In 2004, he realized the need for an unsupervised AI system that could learn from the data and re-program itself to make better predictions. It took him and his partner Steve Jacobs another decade to fine-tune the system and prepare it for real-world investing. Finally, in June 2015, the plan was run for a full day to predict the next day's outcome of the S&P 500. The results, which are proprietary secrets, took them by surprise. In Glickman's own admission, they were able to build artificial superintelligence that could practically beat the market. Apparently, they found the holy grail of stock investing.

This is the story of J4 Capital, an AI-based investment firm from Illinois. J4 is not the only firm in pursuit of building AI systems that can beat the market and generate higher returns from stock investing. Aidyia Holdings, Cerebellum Capital, Taaffeite Capital Management, and Numerai are other examples of AI-driven investment funds.

There's no shortage of skeptics who believe that investing is a specialized and exclusive human domain. However, AI advocates like Glickman believe that AI systems can better analyze past data, find patterns, discern the complexities of the market, and even churn out meaningful information from noise - news headlines, social media posts, and soundbites.

Investment firms, banks, and stock brokers are increasingly equipping investors with AI tools to make more profitable investing decisions. These systems are designed to automatically crunch large volumes of data, identify investment opportunities, predict market moves, execute buy/sell orders, and even manage risks. They don't need to be specifically programmed to do all these - as in J4's case, the machines can potentially learn to do the required on their own. Moreover, they are lightning-fast, easy to access, and don't require technical know-how to make investing decisions. The Davids and Goliaths of the industry - starting from gigantic hedge funds to the do-it-yourself retail investors - all can potentially benefit from AI applications.

A recent survey by a London-based market intelligence firm Market Makers found that 9 out of 10 hedge funds managers would use AI to maximize portfolio returns in 2023. The survey was conducted on 50 portfolio managers from leading hedge funds like Jane Street, Barclays, HSBC, Apollo, and Bridgewater Associates. According to Wall Street data, in 2018 itself 60-73% of equity trading in the US was done using some form of AI.

Time and again, it has been proclaimed that successful stock market investing involves analysis of relevant information, following investing principles, and controlling emotional bias. Machines can crunch data infinitely faster and more efficiently than humans, follow instructions to the T, and displays no emotional vulnerabilities. Can they beat human beings in investing and trading? Let's explore.

Algorithmic trading, automated trading, and high-frequency trading

AI-assisted investing and trading is an evolving domain. Let's look at some of its current avatars.

Algorithmic trading, also known as algo-trading or black-box trading, uses a computer program to execute buy/sell orders using predetermined instructions like price level, time, volume, or the percentage of market movement. For example, suppose you want to buy a certain quantity of all the 30 stocks on the Dow Jones whenever the index corrects by 10%. In that case, you can instruct the algo-trading system the same, and it will execute the order whenever the conditions are fulfilled. So, you don't need to actively track the market to get your preferred price.

The primary idea behind algo-trading is that computers can track a large volume of data, price movements, and technical signals better than human beings. Advanced algo-trading systems track millions of data points, conduct sentiment analysis, and make algorithmic predictions to trade the right security at the right time and the right price. Algo-trading is getting immensely popular, especially among new-age traders and investors. According to a report by Allied Market Research, the global algo-trading market was valued at $12.14 billion in 2020. It's projected to reach $31.49 billion by 2028 with a CAGR of 12.7%.

Automated trading is quite similar to algo-trading. These two terms are often used interchangeably. However, one slight difference is that automated trading is designed to completely eliminate human intervention by allowing the system to generate its own trading rules to maximize profits.

In high-frequency trading, repeated buying and selling occurs at lightning speed to profit from minimal price differentials. High-frequency trading needs highly sophisticated computer systems that can identify and execute a trade in fractions of seconds. Institutional investors like hedge funds generally use this type of trading because of the immense computational power required.

Large investment firms are the first to leverage AI in managing their portfolio because they have substantial financial resources to build a gigantic computing infrastructure. However, various platforms like Trade Ideas, Trend Spider, Tickeron, and Kevout are making AI tools accessible to individual investors at an affordable price.

How AI can help in investing

Profitable investing has long been considered an art that can only be learned after years of first-hand experience. However, AI seems to be challenging this age-old proposition. To summarise, let's look at the precise ways you can use AI to better your investment results.

Better insights and investing ideas

Investment legends like Warren Buffett and Peter Lynch of the world have long advised us first to research what we are investing in. However, with the fast-pacing investing environment in which a humongous amount of information is generated every minute, it's becoming a difficult task for a human investor to keep track of all relevant information. Also, it's increasingly difficult to separate the wheat from the chaff in this age of cacophonous social media and mushrooming online platforms.

Presumably, AI does these tasks better. It has better data-crunching capabilities of churning through a voluminous amount of data to determine what is important. Also, it can track various technical indicators (say, a stock is reaching a 52-week high or trading at record volume) in real-time to generate investing ideas or even buy/sell stocks on your behalf.

Saving time and costs

When stock analysis becomes more straightforward and automated, and you don't need to search for information manually, it saves a lot of time and money. AI can replace your investment advisor. You can simply subscribe to a platform like Trade Ideas, scan for stocks that match your requirements, look for technical indicators for the right time and price to buy/sell, and even back-test your idea with historical data. All these are made possible because of AI and machine learning.

Sentiment analysis

One doesn't need to be an ace investor to realize the importance of sentiment in investing. The real world is in a state of flux, with small and large events constantly shaping economic sentiments that affect investment prospects. Recently we have seen Russia's muscle-flexing on Ukraine put defense stocks on steroids.

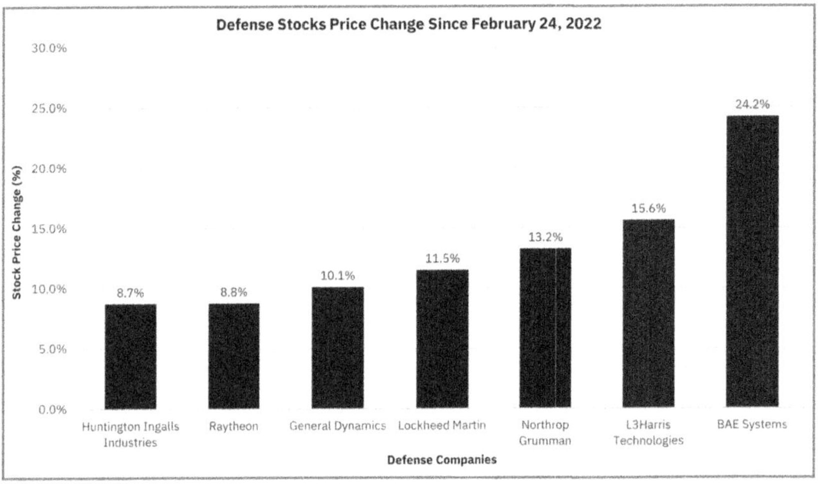

Figure 32: *Price changes in major defence stocks between February 2022 and February 2023 (Source: GlobalData)*

Similarly, economic outlook, geopolitical equations, and investors' sentiment surveys affect investment decision or the relative attractiveness of sectors. It can be too overwhelming for investors to make sense of all this noise and devise optimal investing strategies.

Natural language processing (NLP), one of the most popular applications of AI, can do this task better. NLP tools can analyze gigantic amounts of text to gauge sentiment and boil it down to easily digestible investing guides for us. In the words of John Flowers, CEO and CIO of Next Alpha, a firm depending heavily on AI to invest, *I believed if you could capture every blog, every analyst report, and every chart, and feed it into a machine learning system if you could get all of that, you could measure the emotional index and the velocity of interest people have in different stocks and build a successful trading system.* Interestingly, Next Alpha generated a 42% return for investors compared to 28.8% by the S&P 500 in 2019.

But can everyone become winners?

The investing world is a highly competitive space. If any investing technique, system, or application has an edge over others and beats the overall market, it will soon be used by others. So, over time the competitive advantage of the system would vanish. This has happened with many technical indicators which eventually failed to outperform.

If an AI system consistently outperforms the market - there would be two possibilities. First - the system would be a closely-guarded secret by the owners, much like the quantitative investing secrets of Jim Simons' Medallion Fund which generated an annualized 62% return between 1988 and 2021 - the best in history. Second - everyone else would be using the system, which would eventually remove the advantage. So, we can safely say that while AI can make investing more manageable, accessible, and simplified for ordinary investors, it may not provide the promised market-beating results to everyone. Also, when machines are the only market participants, there will be an infinite loop of complexity in which one machine tries to predict the actions of others in a race to outperform each other. And what about the potential technical glitches that AI can introduce in investing? In one such event in May 2010, the Dow Jones plunged nearly 9% in minutes, mainly caused by algorithmic selling pressure.

It's beyond doubt that AI applications can significantly assist in analyzing information, navigating through increasing complexities, and automating many manual tasks. Moreover, it's prudent to say that an intelligent investor would mix human judgment and AI tools to devise the right investing strategies that suit one's risk appetite, investment goals, and market realities.

So, can AI make you a better investor? The short answer is that it depends on how efficiently you can use AI to your advantage in comparison with other investors. When we asked the same question to ChatGPT, it gave us a quite predictable answer - *it's a challenging goal and past performance is not a guarantee of future results.*

KEY TAKEAWAYS

- AI-assisted investing and trading tools are becoming increasingly popular, as they can analyze past data, find patterns, and discern complexities in the market. They are also capable of processing large volumes of data and identifying investment opportunities.
- Potential technical glitches and the infinite loop of complexity can pose challenges in AI-driven investing and trading. The key to becoming a better investor using AI lies in efficiently utilizing AI tools in combination with human judgment to devise suitable strategies.

Chapter 11

ARE AI COMPANIES IMMUNE TO INFLATION?

Inflation is when you pay fifteen dollars for the ten-dollar haircut you used to get for five dollars when you had hair
*- **Sam Ewing (1920-2001)**, American writer and humorist.*

It isn't typical for the world's largest food and beverages company to miss earnings expectations. Yet, for the year 2022, Nestle reported a lower-than-expected net profit of 9.3 billion Swiss francs compared to analysts' forecasts of 11.6 billion francs. The gross margin, too fell by 260 basis points (2.6%) for the full year. In the words of Bruno Monteyne, MD and senior analyst at Bernstein, *Nestle rarely misses and that was a miss.*

More interestingly, even though the profit fell, the company reported an 8.4% increase in sales for the year. According to Mark Schneider, Nestle's CEO, the steady rise in the price of ingredients has put a dent in the net profit even though sales were higher. The company was forced to increase prices by 8.2% in 2022 to offset the increased commodity costs; however, the pricing move wasn't sufficient to meet profit expectations.

Nestle wasn't the only firm affected by high inflation in recent years. Companies across industries have been affected by the rising prices of ingredients, energy, transportation, and even labor. World's largest company Apple reported a 13% drop in profits in Q4 2022, mainly because of cost escalation in materials, wages, and logistics. According to a Nikkei Asia report, the production cost of its latest flagship model iPhone 14 has increased by as much as 20% from its predecessor.

Inflation eats corporate profits by increasing costs and driving down demand (faced with higher prices, consumers would postpone purchases or shift to cheaper alternatives). Potentially, inflation can affect all types of industries with varying degrees of magnitude. While non-essential spending like holiday travel is greatly curtailed, necessary goods like food and medicine are relatively immune from the vagaries of inflation. Then some industries may experience a windfall gain due to unexpected price rises. The recent energy price hike following the Russia-Ukraine conflict substantially increased the profitability of oil and gas companies. For example, London-based global energy giant Shell earned $40 billion in profit in 2022 - twice that of 2021 and the highest ever in its 115 years of corporate history!

Now let's look at how inflation can potentially impact emerging technologies like AI. What's the potential impact of inflation on AI companies? Will they gain or lose when the world economy is battling decades-high inflation?

Let's explore.

Inflation, inflation everywhere

Gas prices are so high that even the coronavirus stopped traveling! Well, that was a widely circulated joke on social media - but it aptly describes what inflation does. Inflation occurs when there's a consistent rise in the general price level in an economy. So when there's inflation, almost everything - from salt to software - tends to cost more. Inflation lowers the purchasing power of money. So, people with a fixed income can afford less goods and services than before.

Inflation isn't much of a concern when it's relatively low - i.e. in the range of 2-5%. However, there have been multiple episodes of inflationary spikes (inflation rate above 5%) in the last 8 decades. We are currently living in one such episode that started around mid-2021.

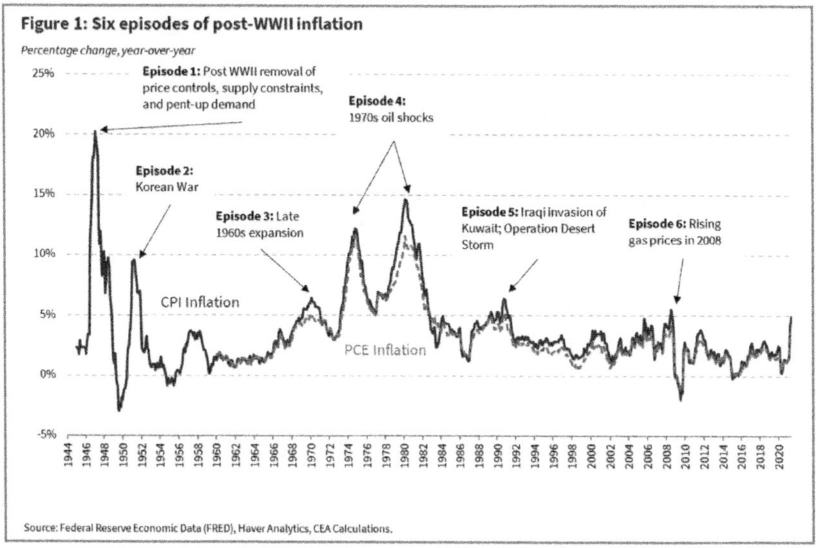

Figure 33: *Inflationary events post World War 2 (Source: Federal Reserve)*

Two of the primary causes of inflation are a consistent rise in the money supply (central banks printing more money to stimulate the economy) and a fall in production (demand exceeds supply). In the last few years, we have seen a confluence of these two factors pushing the overall price level of almost all goods and services to record-high levels.

Between 2020-2022, central banks across the world increased the money supply at a record speed to deal with the pandemic-induced economic slumps. The M2 money supply (measures the readily available stock of money) in the US increased from $15.5 trillion in February 2020 to an all-time high of $21.84 trillion in January 2022. This was an equivalent amount of increase in the previous 8 years. When a higher quantity of money chases the same or even lower quantity of goods (the US GDP fell by 8.9% in Q2 2020 due to the pandemic) the result is an increased price level.

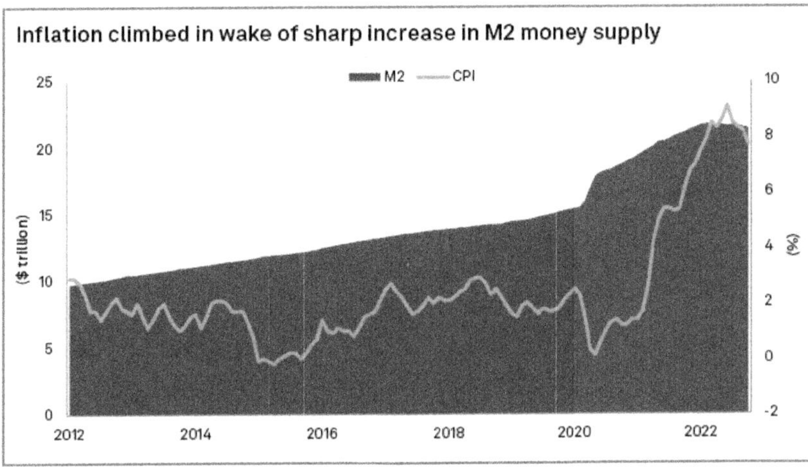

Figure 34: Inflation and M2 money supply between 2012 and 2022 (Source: Federal Reserve)

Moreover, production and supply were badly disrupted first by the lockdowns during the pandemic and then by the US-China trade war and the Russia-Ukraine conflict. Supply bottlenecks of essential commodities - from wheat to oil - led to cost escalation and higher prices of output. In June 2022, the US inflation rate, measured by consumer prices, peaked at a four-decade high of 9.1% before settling at 6.5% by the end of the year.

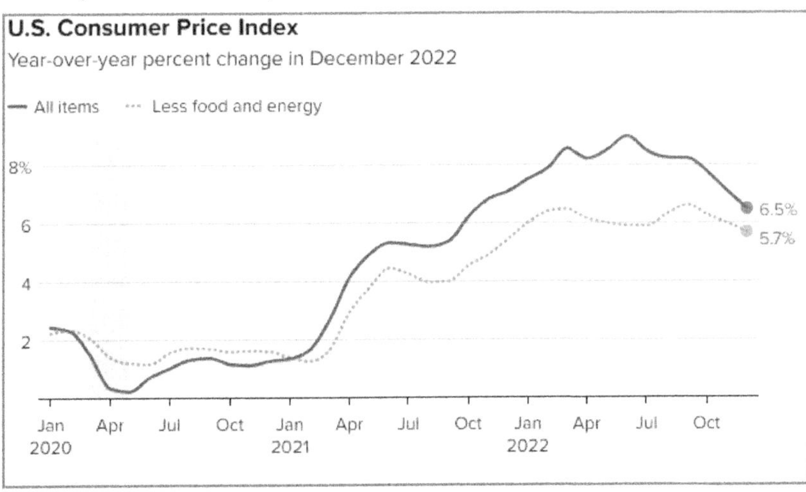

Figure 35: Consumer Price Index between January 2020 and December 2022 (Source: US Bureau of Labor Statistics)

UK inflation reached an even higher level of 11.1% by October 2022 before marginally falling to 10.1 % by January 2023. Compare these figures to the 1960-2021 average inflation rate of 5.1% and 3.8% in the UK and the US respectively. The ongoing episode of abnormal price rise will continue for some time given geopolitical tensions and supply bottlenecks.

The potential cost of inflation to the AI Industry

Without much pretension, let's admit that inflation indeed has certain potentially adverse effects on the overall AI industry. Let's look at each of those.

Higher costs

When the general price level is higher, companies need to pay a higher amount for all their inputs - be it hardware, software, office essentials, or even employee wages. According to data compiled by IDC, a leading global market intelligence firm, between 2020 and 2022 there was an average 18-20% rise in prices of laptops/PCs, a 10-15% rise in server and storage costs, and a 5-7% rise in enterprise software pricing. These price hikes can substantially increase the operating costs of AI companies.

Lower demand

When operating costs are higher, an AI company would be forced to pass some of these increased costs to customers by hiking the final price of its offerings. For example, IT major CISCO, which has an elaborate AI software and hardware portfolio, increased its prices by 10% in 2022. The higher prices are likely to drive away some customers resulting in lower demand and lower revenue.

Lower profitability

Higher costs and lower demand would automatically put pressure on the bottom line of an AI company. Lower profits translate into lower investor confidence, a reduced capability to invest in growth-inducing technologies, and limited expansion capabilities. Also, long-term survival would be greatly challenged if an AI company cannot generate a consistent profit. Moreover, as AI is an emerging technology and many companies in this field are start-ups, lower profit prospects would destabilize the industry's future growth.

Reduced funding

When the inflation rate is high, one of the first things the central bank (the primary custodian of an economy's macroeconomic stability) would do is increase the interest rates. During the COVID crisis, the US Fed cut the interest rate to near zero. However, record inflation forced the central bank to take a hawkish stance. The Fed raised the benchmark interest rate 8 times (another record) between March 2022 and February 2023 bringing it to the range of 4.50%-4.75%. Further rate increases can't be discarded at this moment. Other major central banks like the European Central Bank (ECB) and Bank of England (BOE) have taken similar tightening policies to ease inflation.

When the interest rates go up, borrowing becomes costlier. This can dry up investment in emerging technologies as they are riskier while investors may be looking for assured higher returns. Moreover, a high-interest environment is unfavorable for the equity markets as fixed-income securities like government bonds can fetch better returns. Therefore, higher interest rates can depress the stock prices of AI companies.

Uncertainty and difficulty in forecasting

One of the biggest business costs of inflation is the uncertainty it creates for companies. Since inflation is a primary macroeconomic factor, it can adversely affect the whole economy and trigger a chain reaction. As we discussed in the previous point, higher inflation leads to higher interest rates which can diminish investment prospects and raise the probability of a recession.

When business uncertainties increase, AI companies could find it difficult to make strategic plans and investment decisions. Moreover, financial uncertainties are likely to make investors develop cold feet and postpone funding until there's greater clarity.

There's some great news too

Empowering businesses with hyperlearning - bringing together human, machine, and organizational learning - reads the motto of Symson, a Rotterdam-based AI firm. Founded in 2018 as a spin-off (when a subsidiary becomes a separate company) from the Erasmus University Rotterdam, Symson specializes in developing pricing strategies for companies using specialized AI tools.

Faced with high inflation, companies' primary goals are to minimize costs and price their offerings to maximize net profit. Symson's products are highly suited for such companies looking for price optimization in an inflationary environment. Symson is one of the hundreds of AI-based firms which are empowering businesses to deal with inflation by minimizing costs, developing competitive pricing, automating processes, removing redundancies, and achieving overall efficiency.

In short, the good news is that when it comes to inflation, AI companies have a huge untapped market. If rising inflation is a crisis, firms need to innovate more to cut costs and protect profits. Therefore, it would be a strategic move for firms to integrate AI tools into their core business processes. According to Alexander Bant, Practice Vice President, Finance at Gartner - *CFOs must try to lead the C-suite to drive a unified enterprise digital strategy. Inflation can be a catalyst for organizations to drive key digital and cost-reduction initiatives across the whole business.* When industries buy more AI solutions, the revenue of AI companies will increase substantially. These companies are uniquely positioned to help firms navigate the inflationary market through cost optimization, optimal resource management, automation, elimination of wastage, reduction of the product development cycle, and better consumer insights. AI companies are helping firms across industries - from biotechnology to software development - optimize processes and reduce costs.

In July 2022, Morgan Stanley released a 60-page research paper titled *The Deflation Enablers.* In the report, the consulting major highlighted the importance of firms spending on technologies that would *increase productivity, lower costs, and improve profitability.*

Figure 36: *Index of deflation enablers vs. MSCI World in 2022 (Source: Morgan Stanley)*

Morgan Stanley calls these technologies deflation enablers or antidotes to inflation. This list of deflation enablers mentions AI at the top, followed by clean energy and mass energy storage. These technologies enable companies to increase productivity, achieve a declining cost curve, and maintain competitive strength. The report shows these deflation enablers are grossly undervalued compared to the MSCI World Index (a broad global equity index consisting of major stocks from 23 developed markets). Utilizing this report, AI companies can be considerable benefactors in this inflationary environment both from an investment point of view and from the perspective of facing increased demand for their products.

Coming back to the important question - so, are AI companies immune to inflation? The answer is that while high inflation presents both difficulties and opportunities for AI companies, the latter can potentially outweigh the former by a huge margin. It's up to individual AI companies - how they exploit the market potential while navigating through the challenges.

KEY TAKEAWAYS

- ◇ Inflation can lead to higher operating costs, lower demand, reduced profitability, and less funding for AI companies.
- ◇ Businesses can leverage AI to help deal with inflation. AI can be used to optimize costs, automate processes, and increase efficiency.
- ◇ According to Morgan Stanley's research, AI is a key deflation enabler making AI-focused companies potentially valuable investments in the current inflationary environment.

Chapter 12

FINDING A BALANCE: THE ROLE OF AI REGULATIONS IN ENSURING ETHICAL AND SAFE USE OF TECHNOLOGY

Success in creating AI would be the biggest event in human history. Unfortunately, it might also be the last, unless we learn how to avoid the risks.
- Stephen Hawking.

Since 2014, machine learning experts at Amazon, the world's largest online retailer, have been developing an AI application to simplify the company's recruitment system. The goal was to build a system to automate the job application review process. Over the years, Amazon has been hugely successful in leveraging AI to automate different aspects of its operations - managing warehouses, driving the supply chain, or even developing pricing strategies. So, extending the same expertise to its recruitment processes was a natural step for the company. The AI-based recruitment system was supposed to rate candidates on a scale of 1 to 5 based on their experience and skills after going through the resumes. According to a company insider familiar with this project, *everyone wanted this holy grail. They literally wanted it to be an engine where I'm going to give you 100 resumes, it will spit out the top five, and we'll hire those.* Things were going fine until 2015 when the managers observed something strange - the application seemed to have a dislike for women!

It started becoming evident that the system was not recommending candidates for certain jobs, especially the ones requiring technical skills, in a gender-neutral way. The recruitment system preferred men over women in those job categories irrespective of the degrees or prior experience of the applicants. It underrated the resumes that mentioned the words *woman, women's college, or women's clubs.* Further investigation found that the problem was in the training data that included the previous 10 years of recruitment patterns and resumes submitted. At Amazon, like most other companies, men tend to outnumber women in technical posts by a significant margin. Naturally, the predictions of the machines are no better than the quality of the training date - bias in, bias out. Specialists tried to retrain the system to remove the bias. However, the company ultimately disbanded the system in 2017 after losing hope of creating a perfect recruitment system.

AI, predicted to become a $15.7 trillion industry by 2030, is far from perfect. Predictions by AI systems can be racially discriminatory, gender-biased, misleading, incomplete, or even outright wrong. AI systems are only as good as the data used to train them. The training data can contain bias, inaccuracies, and prejudices which would be reflected in the predictions of an AI system.

A recent joint study by researchers from the University of Washington, Carnegie Mellon University, and the Allen Institute for Artificial Intelligence found that tweets by African Americans are 1.5 times more likely to be tagged as offensive by leading AI models identifying hate speeches on social media. According to a report by the National Institute of Standards and Technology, researchers evaluated predictions by 189 AI-based facial recognition systems. The study found that Black and Asian faces were 10 to 100 times more likely to be identified as criminals than white faces. We have recently seen multiple media reports of ChatGPT giving wrong answers, quite confidently, to basic arithmetic questions. Given this reality, how can we completely rely on AI to flag hate speeches, evaluate job applications, assist in airport security, prevent crimes, communicate with customers, or develop bias-free content? Also, where would be the limit of AI developments?

Who would ensure that AI technologies wouldn't be used to develop weapons of mass destruction or similar dangerous tools?

If AI has to be the central driving force of the future economy or the larger society, there needs to be an effective solution to all these menaces. Since AI holds the unbound future potential to benefit all spheres of humanity, altogether banning AI developments is already out of the question. Therefore, there's a rising demand for comprehensive regulatory policies to ensure AI applications maximize the benefits for humanity while getting rid of the adverse effects. Countries around the world are working on norms and laws to regulate AI in the immediate future. However, there are certain potential challenges to AI regulations, so let's look at those.

Challenges in regulating AI

The word regulation is defined by the Oxford English Dictionary as *explicit rules to govern behaviour that are enforced by specified institutions or agencies.* Now, if we want to govern the behavior of AI systems, we are taking up a highly challenging task.

One of the central problems in regulating AI is that many of its predictions are not explainable. For example, we can't know how the applications arrive at a certain decision. In technical terms, this is called the *Black Box problem.* Since many of the AI models are designed to learn from the data to make predictions, it's not directly observable how the machine chooses certain predictions over others. Therefore, it's tough to audit or filter AI systems - let alone predict their outcomes. In short, we don't know when the next outcome is going to be inaccurate, incomplete, or biased until the outcome has already occurred and the harm has been done.

Secondly, while it's true that the quality of the training data affects the predictions of an AI system, it's another challenge to ensure the training data is free from all sorts of errors and biases. The problem is even amplified given the immense volume of data required to train AI foundation models (like ChatGPT and Google's Bard). A large portion of this data is human-generated texts likely to contain human bias. Cleaning such a large amount of data can raise the cost of training AI models to a prohibitively high level. Moreover, cleaning such a gigantic amount of data may be infeasible in many cases.

Thirdly, AI models are not static - they are designed to learn and improve continuously to refine the predictions as more users use them. This also means the predictions would evolve and the same query can result in different forecasts at different points in time. Regulating a dynamic system with a static set of regulations will be another challenge.

Potential implications of AI regulations

In February 2023, Time magazine asked Mira Maruti, the Chief Technology Officer at OpenAI and a key architect of ChatGPT, about the need for AI regulations. In her own words, *AI can be misused, or it can be used by bad actors. So, then there are questions about how you govern the use of this technology globally. How do you govern the use of AI in a way that's aligned with human values?* She went on to add - *we need a ton more input in this system and a lot more input that goes beyond the technologies-—definitely regulators and governments and everyone else.* Clearly, there cannot be better advocates of the requirement for a comprehensive regulatory framework to govern AI than the movers and shakers of the industry itself. However, AI regulations would come at certain unavoidable costs for AI companies.

When it comes to AI regulations, the EU has shown leadership by proposing the Artificial Intelligence Act (AI Act) in April 2021. One of the stated goals of the Act is to ensure that *AI works for people and is a force for good in society.* The Federal Trade Commission (FTC) in the USA has also released policy papers on AI regulations. As leading AI models become increasingly popular, we can expect rapid progress in the enforcement of these regulatory policies. One of the potential implications of these regulations on AI companies would be the increased cost and time required to train AI models. For example, the EU's AI Act mentions that *training, validation, and testing datasets shall be relevant, representative, free of errors, and complete.* However, given the gigantic size of the training dataset, it would be a herculean task for AI companies to meet all these requirements. Clearly, the cost and cycle time of the models are bound to rise substantially. Moreover, some AI companies may be forced to retrain their models from scratch with new datasets. So, these regulations can potentially create a huge speed breaker on the path of rapid innovation.

Another potential regulatory impact can originate from asymmetric regulations like different regulatory norms in other countries or regions. It can create disadvantages for companies located in stricter jurisdictions compared to companies located in places where the regulations are relatively lax. For example, the EU's strict data privacy law General Data Protection Regulation (GDPR) puts European companies in a relatively disadvantageous position relative to their Chinese counterparts who face relatively less strict regulations.

Moreover, regulations are bound to increase compliance costs for AI companies as failure to comply will attract steep penalties. Companies would be forced to conduct periodic compliance audits to ensure they are not in violation of any of the regulatory norms.

Given the current developments, stricter AI regulations are likely to be a reality in the near future, in spite of their impacts like increased costs or a lower rate of innovation. Going forward, AI companies will have to find ways to innovate and optimize costs while complying with an increasing number of regulations.

KEY TAKEAWAYS

- ◇ Outputs from AI models can be discriminatory, biased or even outright false. So there is an argument for needing comprehensive regulations to ensure AI applications benefit humanity while minimizing adverse effects.
- ◇ Regulating AI is challenging due to the "Black Box" problem – which is the lack of transparency on how AI algorithms reach their decisions.
- ◇ The EU has proposed the Artificial Intelligence Act to govern AI, but enforcing these regulations may increase costs and time required to train AI models and therefore create competitive disadvantages for companies in stricter jurisdictions.

CONCLUSION

The opening paragraph of this book cited John Doerr's quote about how the internet would be the "largest legal creation of wealth in history."

Now let's fast forward to the present day and another prediction from a renowned investor. In March 2023, Doug Leone of Seqouia Capital, a man Forbes cited as one of the top 10 technology investors on the planet, said this about AI.

"AI is the next platform shift, in the same way that mobile was the one before, and the same way the internet was the one before that. That being said, we're going to overestimate it in the short term. We're going to invest in everything, in the same way that in 1999 we invested in everything.
So you have to have a good head on your shoulders, where you don't practice FOMO, where you don't chase every company just because everyone else is."

Leone's comments are a mirror of Amara's Law. A maxim which states that we overestimate the effects of a technology in the short term, but underestimate its effects in the long run.

So even though it may not feel like it, we are still very much in the early stages of AI on both a technological level, and on an investing level in the public markets. You will see companies throwing out terms like "AI enabled" and "AI powered" in their earnings reports. You will see more companies with AI in their name going public despite minimal revenues, or even no revenue at all.

That's precisely why in this book we've taken a more pragmatic approach to investing in AI companies at this present point. In the public markets, the concentration of wealth is likely to be focused on established cloud-computing providers (Amazon, Google, Microsoft), hardware manufacturers (Nvidia, Intel) and companies that have large datasets to work with (Meta, Perion). That's not to say that the next Google, Amazon or Facebook won't come out of the AI revolution, it's just far too early to tell.

What we do know is that a repeat of the markets we saw individual investors make in recent investing trends like electric vehicles and blockchain, are sure to lose you money. So as always, our golden rule of investing is this

Don't invest in anything that you don't understand

It's a simple mantra, but it is the easiest way to combat FOMO and other bad investing habits.

I hope we've armed you with the skillset needed not only to understand investing in AI companies, but also to profit long-term from this megatrend.

However if there is something you don't understand, you can email us at admin@freemanpublications.com. We answer every single reader's email.

2022 was a chaotic year, so as we move into 2023, we wish you the best of luck with your investing!

One final word from us. If this book has helped you in any way, we'd appreciate it if you left a review on Amazon.

Reviews are the lifeblood of our business. We read every single one and incorporate your feedback into our future book projects.

To leave an Amazon review, go to https://freemanpublications.com/leaveareview.

Bonus Chapter

USING AI TOOLS TO SPEED UP YOUR INVESTING RESEARCH

Since the release of ChatGPT Plus in February 2023, I've been using it, along with some other AI tools, to speed up my investing research process.

We systemize our entire process into a repeatable framework inside our Capital Gains Multiplier program. This framework aims to ensure that you can discover all the information you need about a company in the least amount of time possible.

Now with the aid of AI, we can accelerate this process even more by using tools like ChatGPT. So in this bonus chapter, I'll show you exactly how I'm using it.

Industry Overviews

Some industries tend to be more complex than others, particularly if you don't have a professional background inside them. 2 such industries are semiconductors and cybersecurity where there are a number of different elements to them, and companies which specialize in different segments.

When doing a deep dive on Crowdstrike for our members, one of them asked me how Crowdstrike differs from other public companies like Palo Alto Networks. If you wanted to see this for yourself, a ChatGPT prompt could be as follows.

What are the different components of [industry]? Use [public company names] in your examples

Here is ChatGPT's response to that question

The cybersecurity industry encompasses various components, with specialized companies addressing distinct security aspects:

1. Network Security: Safeguards network infrastructure from unauthorized access and threats.
   - Fortinet: Network security appliances (firewalls, IPS, secure access)
   - Palo Alto Networks: Next-gen firewalls, threat intelligence, cloud security
2. Identity & Access Management (IAM): Manages user identities, authentication, and authorization.
   - Okta: Single sign-on, multi-factor authentication, identity lifecycle management
3. Content Delivery & Security: Distributes and secures online content while defending against DDoS attacks and threats.
   - Cloudflare: CDN, DDoS protection, web application firewalls
   - Fastly: Edge computing, CDN, web application firewalls
4. Cloud Security: Addresses security challenges in cloud environments (data protection, access control, compliance).
   - ZScaler: Cloud-based security (secure web gateways, CASB, ZTNA)
5. Security Monitoring & Analytics: Collects and analyzes security data for threat detection and response.
   - Datadog: Cloud-scale application observability, security monitoring, threat detection
6. Endpoint Security: Protects end-user devices from malware, exploits, and threats.
   - CrowdStrike: Cloud-native endpoint protection (antivirus, EDR, threat hunting)
   - SentinelOne: AI-driven endpoint security (prevention, detection, response, hunting)

As you can see, we instantly get an overview of the different companies in the cybersecurity industry and which ones can be considered direct competitors to one another.

Now we have more context when it comes to areas like growth rates, margins and valuation because I can focus on comparing Crowdstrike to a direct peer like SentinelOne.

Economic moats

A company's lasting competitive advantage, also known as its economic moat, is one of the more difficult concepts to understand for new investors. So much so that we wrote an entire book about it called **Fantastic Moats and Where to Find Them**

Fortunately, with ChatGPT we can quickly get a high-level overview of a company's economic moat by using the following prompt

What is [company name's] economic moat? Do not include subjective concepts like "expertise" or "skilled workforce"

Here are the results for Crowdstrike

1. Proprietary Technology: Crowdstrike's Falcon platform is a cloud-native, endpoint security solution that differentiates the company from competitors that rely on legacy systems or hybrid solutions. Its cloud-native architecture allows for easy scalability and rapid updates, providing an edge in the ever-evolving cybersecurity landscape.
2. Strong Brand and Reputation: Crowdstrike has built a strong reputation for effectively responding to and mitigating high-profile cyberattacks. This reputation enhances customer trust and confidence, which can be a significant advantage in the competitive cybersecurity market.
3. Network Effect: As more customers use Crowdstrike's platform, the company collects and analyzes a vast amount of data on cyber threats. This data enables Crowdstrike to continuously improve its threat detection and prevention capabilities, making the platform more effective and valuable for its customers. The network effect also acts as a barrier to entry for new competitors, as it would be difficult for them to match the scale and effectiveness of Crowdstrike's platform.
4. High Customer Switching Costs: Once an organization has implemented a cybersecurity solution like Crowdstrike's Falcon platform, it can be costly and time-consuming to switch to a different provider. This creates a certain level of customer stickiness and reduces the likelihood of customer churn, which helps to protect Crowdstrike's market share.

From this list of 4 points, the network effects and high switching costs are certainly the 2 strongest arguments that Crowdstrike does indeed have an economic moat.

Reverse thesis

One factor that plagues investors, especially newer ones, is being blinded by the bull case for a company. As much as we try to be impartial and actively look for red flags, our brains can sometimes gloss over details which don't fit our narrative. Fortunately, we can ask ChatGPT to provide us with an impartial analysis for the reverse of our thesis. Here is the prompt I would use for that.

I want you to act as an investment manager who has a fiduciary duty to advise clients impartially. Knowing this, outline a potential bear thesis for [company name] (company ticker symbol)

At the time of writing, ChatGPT's dataset cutoff is September 2021, so some elements of the response may need to be fact-checked. Here is the response to the above question for Crowdstrike.

Bear Thesis for Crowdstrike (CRWD):

1. High Valuation: As of my knowledge cutoff in September 2021, Crowdstrike had a relatively high valuation, which could be a potential concern for investors. The price-to-sales (P/S) and price-to-earnings (P/E) ratios were considerably higher than industry averages, which could indicate that the stock is overvalued. If market sentiment changes or growth slows, the stock price could experience significant declines.
2. Competition: The cybersecurity industry is highly competitive, with numerous established players like Microsoft, Palo Alto Networks, and Fortinet, as well as emerging companies. Increased competition could put pressure on Crowdstrike's market share, pricing power, and customer acquisition, which may impact its growth trajectory and profitability.
3. Customer Concentration: Crowdstrike's revenue is generated from a relatively small number of large customers, which can pose a risk to the stability of its earnings. If the company were to lose a significant customer, it could have a material impact on its financial performance.
4. Economic Downturns: In the event of an economic downturn or a slowdown in IT spending, organizations may opt to cut back on their cybersecurity budgets or delay new investments. This could negatively impact Crowdstrike's revenue growth and profitability.
5. Regulatory Risks: Changes in data privacy regulations or increased scrutiny of cybersecurity practices could potentially impact the demand for Crowdstrike's products and services. Additionally, the company may face increased compliance costs, which could affect its profitability.
6. Execution Risks: Crowdstrike's ability to maintain its growth trajectory depends on its ability to successfully execute its business strategies, such as international expansion, new product development, and customer retention. Any missteps in execution or failure to meet growth targets could negatively impact investor sentiment and the company's stock price.

As you can see here, ChatGPT gives us 6 points which could be of potential concern. It's important to stress to not take any of the outputs at face value, and you must fact check all the data ChatGPT responds with, primarily because, at the time of writing, ChatGPT does not have access to the internet.

This is why we use the reverse thesis prompt at the end of our research, not at the beginning. For example, after doing my due diligence on Crowdstrike, I know Risk Fact #3 "customer concentration" is not valid, as, in the latest financial year, the company does not have any single customer, which generates more than 10% of the company's total revenue.

How do I know this? Well it's thanks to a simple AI tool called "AskYourPDF"

If you've ever done thorough research on a company, you've no doubt looked at a 10-K form. For the unaware, this is the annual report that the SEC requires every public company to file. You'll be overwhelmed at first if you've never read one. They tend to be 100+ pages long (Crowdstrike's is 138) and chock full of corporate speak.

We look at 10-K forms because they are the best source of truth when it comes to a company's genuine prospects. This is because the SEC requires companies to list details like risk factors, legal proceedings as well as audited financial data.

But thanks to askyourpdf.com – we can get the answers to questions much quicker.

Ask Your PDF

This is a website where you can upload any PDF and then use a chatbot to ask questions about data inside the document. The website is free and you don't need to give an email address to use the tool. For us as investors, this is incredibly useful as it helps us to quickly get answers to precise questions.

Before you rush ahead and ask if Crowdstrike is worth investing in, it's essential to know that this tool only works if you request questions with Yes/No answers, or questions that do not require any nuance or subjectivity to an answer.

Question that works well: Does Crowdstrike have customer concentration risk?

Question that doesn't work: What is the biggest risk to Crowdstrike as a company?

Does Crowdstrike have customer concentration risk?

According to the "Notes to Consolidated Financial Statements" provided, the company does not have customer concentration risk. As of January 31, 2023, there were no direct customers who represented 10% or more of the Company's accounts receivable. One direct customer who represented 10% or more of the Company's accounts receivable as of January 31, 2022, was listed as "Customer A" and represented 9% of the accounts receivable.

Other questions which work well for a 10-K form:

- Are there any legal proceedings against [company name]?
- How does [company name] protect its intellectual property?
- Who are [company name's] main competitors?
- Is [company name's] founder still actively involved with the company?
- Has [company name] experienced any weakness within its financial reporting?
- Is [company name] planning to do any share buybacks or issue a dividend?
- What was [company name's] revenue/earnings growth rate last year?
- Has [company name] made any significant acquisitions in the last year?
- Does [company name] have more cash or debt?
- What is the breakdown of [company name's] revenue?
- What sources of revenue does [company name] have?
- Has [company name] issued more shares in the last year?

These are the questions we currently use in our company research framework. And as AI technology continues to develop, we'll share more of our findings with our members. If you'd like to know more about our program, which has helped over 220 students accelerate their journey to financial freedom...

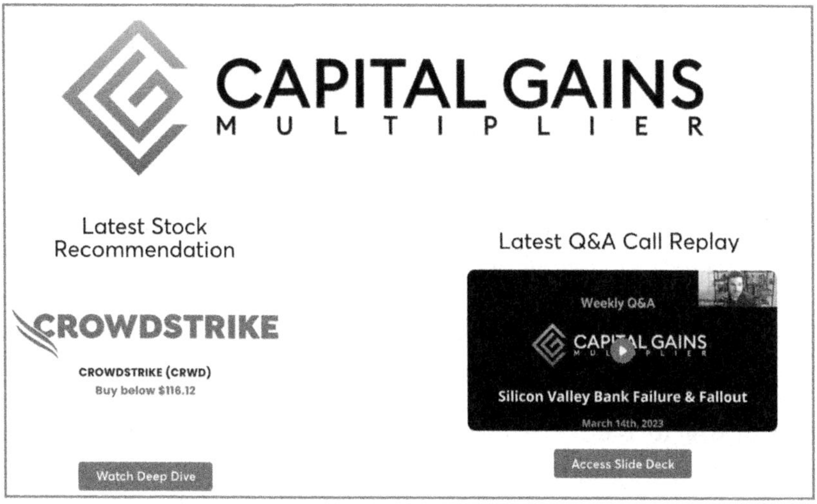

Go to **<u>freemanpublications.com/chat</u>**

ACKNOWLEDGEMENTS

This book is a team effort, and while I get to be the face of the business and receive all the kind messages from readers, I can't ignore the people who helped make this book what it was.

Thank you first to our content team for their writing, editing, and proofreading efforts and dealing with my persistent questions about specific changes needing to be made.

Thank you to Mark Greenberg, our superstar narrator, who has really become "the voice" of Freeman Publications over the past 3 years.

Thank you to the 520+ Freeman readers who participated in our advanced reader program for this book. Your notes and feedback were invaluable in going from the final draft to the finished product. A special shout out to the readers of Superhuman AI and Ben's Bites – 2 excellent newsletters

A special mention must go to two people. First, Vinay Narayanan for his help on the book content despite travelling to multiple continents, and working all hours of the day. Not only for this book, but to the entire Freeman community as a whole.

Then Carlota Wilhite for her incredibly detailed feedback, ranging from areas we didn't clarify well enough to pointing out that one of my original chapter titles was immature! Without your input, this book simply would not have been as good as it is today.

An additional thank you to our thousands of readers on social media for your words of encouragement throughout this project.

Finally, thank you to my family, whose initial uncertainty of "are you still doing that book thing" has blossomed into full support for my vision here at Freeman Publications. This means more than you will ever know.

Oliver

London, England
April 2023

REFERENCES

4 types of artificial intelligence. Built In. (2022, August). Retrieved March 2, 2023, from https://builtin.com/artificial-intelligence/types-of-artificial-intelligence

5 factors of technology adoption rates. On Digital Marketing. (2015, July 24). Retrieved March 3, 2023, from https://ondigitalmarketing.com/learn/odm/foundations/5-factors-that-influence-technology-adoption-rates/

Abhishek, K. (2022, May 10). Introduction to artificial intelligence. Simple Talk. Retrieved March 2, 2023, from https://www.red-gate.com/simple-talk/development/data-science-development/introduction-to-artificial-intelligence/

Ai regulation is coming. Harvard Business Review. (2021, August 30). Retrieved March 3, 2023, from https://hbr.org/2021/09/ai-regulation-is-coming

Allied Market Research. (2021, July 8). Global algorithmic trading market to garner $31.49 billion by 2028: Allied Market Research. GlobeNewswire News Room. Retrieved March 3, 2023, from https://www.globenewswire.com/en/news-release/2021/07/08/2259816/0/en/Global-algorithmic-trading-market-to-garner-31-49-billion-by-2028-Allied-Market-Research.html

Alphafold reveals the structure of the protein universe. RSS. (2022, August). Retrieved March 3, 2023, from https://www.deepmind.com/blog/alphafold-reveals-the-structure-of-the-protein-universe

Ariosa, L. L. (2023, January 12). In-memory computing could upend how computers process. IBM Research Blog. Retrieved March 3, 2023, from https://research.ibm.com/blog/abu-sebastian-ieee-in-memory-computing

Artificial Intelligence (AI) market (by offering: Hardware, software, services; by technology: Machine Learning, natural language processing, context-aware computing, Computer Vision; by deployment: On-premise, cloud; by organization size: Large Enterprises, Small & Medium Enterprises; by Business Function: Marketing and sales, security, finance, law, human resource, other; by end-use:) - global industry analysis, size, share, growth, trends, regional outlook, and forecast 2022 – 2030. Precedence Research. (n.d.). Retrieved March 3, 2023, from https://www.precedenceresearch.com/artificial-intelligence-market

Artificial Intelligence Market Size & Share Analysis Report 2030. (n.d.). Retrieved March 3, 2023, from https://www.grandviewresearch.com/industry-analysis/artificial-intelligence-ai-market

BBC. (2014, June 9). Computer AI passes Turing test in 'World First'. BBC News. Retrieved March 2, 2023, from https://www.bbc.com/news/technology-27762088

Babu, S. (2022, February 11). Supervised, unsupervised and semi-supervised learning. OpenGenus IQ: Computing Expertise & Legacy. Retrieved March 2, 2023, from https://iq.opengenus.org/supervised-unsupervised-and-semi-supervised-learning/

Biswal, A. (2023, February 7). Top 18 artificial intelligence (AI) applications in 2023: Simplilearn. Simplilearn.com. Retrieved March 2, 2023, from https://www.simplilearn.com/tutorials/artificial-intelligence-tutorial/artificial-intelligence-applications

Blog, T. P. arX. (2022, February 21). AI machines have beaten Moore's law over the last decade, say computer scientists. Discover Magazine. Retrieved March 3, 2023, from https://www.discovermagazine.com/technology/ai-machines-have-beaten-moores-law-over-the-last-decade-say-computer

Bloomberg. (2022, June 27). $422.37+ Billion global artificial intelligence (AI) market size likely to grow at 39.4% CAGR during 2022-2028 | industry. Bloomberg.com. Retrieved March 2, 2023, from https://www.bloomberg.com/press-releases/2022-06-27/-422-37-billion-global-artificial-intelligence-ai-market-size-likely-to-grow-at-39-4-cagr-during-2022-2028-industry

Brown, M. (2015, July 6). Nikola Tesla predicted smartphones in 1926 like a boss. GeekWire. Retrieved March 3, 2023, from https://www.geekwire.com/2015/nikola-tesla-predicted-smartphones-in-1926-like-a-boss/#:~:text=According%20to%20a%20quote%20found,1926%20interview%20with%20Collier's%20magazine.

Brown, S. (2021, April 21). Machine Learning, explained. MIT Sloan. Retrieved March 2, 2023, from https://mitsloan.mit.edu/ideas-made-to-matter/machine-learning-explained

Cable News Network. (2007, June). IPhone Mania hits flagship stores. CNNMoney. Retrieved March 3, 2023, from https://money.cnn.com/2007/06/29/technology/iphone/

Calvello, A. (2021, February 18). The most powerful artificial intelligence knows nothing about investing. that's perfectly okay. Institutional Investor. Retrieved March 3, 2023, from https://www.institutionalinvestor.com/article/b1qlrt5hr035ds/The-Most-Powerful-Artificial-Intelligence-Knows-Nothing-About-Investing-That-s-Perfectly-Okay

Can artificial intelligence learn to beat the stock market? - fast company. (n.d.). Retrieved March 3, 2023, from https://www.fastcompany.com/90502428/artificial-intelligence-beat-the-stock-market

Chai, W. (2020, October 20). A timeline of machine learning history. WhatIs.com. Retrieved March 2, 2023, from https://www.techtarget.com/whatis/A-Timeline-of-Machine-Learning-History

Cisco Price Increase: How to offset the impact. NPI. (2022, March 14). Retrieved March 3, 2023, from https://npifinancial.com/blog/cisco-price-increase-how-to-offset-the-impact/#:~:text=The%20January%202022%20Cisco%20Price%20Increase&text=In%20partner%20communications%2C%20Cisco%20claimed,including%20SaaS%20%E2%80%93%20will%20be%20exempt.

Company. SYMSON. (n.d.). Retrieved March 3, 2023, from https://www.symson.com/about-us/our-company/company

Dastin, J. (2018, October 10). Amazon scraps secret AI recruiting tool that showed bias against women. Reuters. Retrieved March 3, 2023, from https://www.reuters.com/article/us-amazon-com-jobs-automation-insight-idUSKCN1MK08G

Denton, J. (2023, February 9). The crypto crowd is piling into AI, a possible sign of a bubble. Barron's. Retrieved March 3, 2023, from https://www.barrons.com/articles/ai-stocks-google-bard-chatgpt-crypto-bubble-51675857497

Digital around the world - datareportal – global digital insights. DataReportal. (n.d.). Retrieved March 3, 2023, from https://datareportal.com/global-digital-overview

Dobush, G. (2021, June 8). Why shares of cannabis producer Tilray have gotten very, very high-and why investors think they could crash. Fortune. Retrieved March 3, 2023, from https://fortune.com/2018/09/20/tilray-cannabis-shares-mad-money/

Dow Jones & Company. (2019, April 5). Legalization in Canada sparks rally in marijuana stocks. The Wall Street Journal. Retrieved March 3, 2023, from https://www.wsj.com/articles/legalization-in-canada-sparks-rally-in-marijuana-stocks-11554465600

Economic update: Growth slows as uncertainty rises. (n.d.). Retrieved March 3, 2023, from https://commonslibrary.parliament.uk/economic-update-growth-slows-as-uncertainty-rises/

Electric vehicles - worldwide: Statista market forecast. Statista. (2023, January). Retrieved March 3, 2023, from https://www.statista.com/outlook/mmo/electric-vehicles/worldwide

Elias, J. (2023, February 10). Google employees criticize CEO Sundar Pichai for 'rushed, botched' announcement of GPT competitor Bard. CNBC. Retrieved March 3, 2023, from https://www.cnbc.com/2023/02/10/google-employees-slam-ceo-sundar-pichai-for-rushed-bard-announcement.html

Facial Recognition Technology (FRT). NIST. (2020, February 6). Retrieved March 3, 2023, from https://www.nist.gov/speech-testimony/facial-recognition-technology-frt-0

Frankenfield, J. (2022, November 11). What is a graphics processing unit (GPU)? definition and examples. Investopedia. Retrieved March 3, 2023, from https://www.investopedia.com/terms/g/graphics-processing-unit-gpu.asp#:~:text=Nvidia%20defined%20a%20GPU%20as,by%20optimizing%203D%20gaming%20performance.

Gartner_Inc. (2023, January). Beyond chatgpt: The future of generative AI for enterprises. Gartner. Retrieved March 3, 2023, from https://www.gartner.com/en/articles/beyond-chatgpt-the-future-of-generative-ai-for-enterprises

Gartner_Inc. (n.d.). Gartner predicts the future of AI Technologies. Gartner. Retrieved March 2, 2023, from https://www.gartner.com/smarterwithgartner/gartner-predicts-the-future-of-ai-technologies

Gartner_Inc. (n.d.). How to mitigate inflation in finance transformation. Gartner. Retrieved March 3, 2023, from https://www.gartner.com/en/articles/cfos-use-technology-in-your-inflation-fight

Gartner_Inc. (n.d.). What's new in the 2022 Gartner Hype Cycle for Emerging Technologies. Gartner. Retrieved March 3, 2023, from https://www.gartner.com/en/articles/what-s-new-in-the-2022-gartner-hype-cycle-for-emerging-technologies

Generative AI market size - global industry, share, analysis, trends and forecast 2022 - 2030. Acumen Research and Consulting. (2022, December). Retrieved March 3, 2023, from https://www.acumenresearchandconsulting.com/generative-ai-market

Generative AI. BCG Global. (2023, January). Retrieved March 3, 2023, from https://www.bcg.com/x/artificial-intelligence/generative-ai

Generative models - GitHub Pages. (2019, February). Retrieved March 3, 2023, from https://humboldt-wi.github.io/blog/research/information_systems_1819/generativemodels/

Ghaffary, S. (2019, August 15). The algorithms that detect hate speech online are biased against Black people. Vox. Retrieved March 3, 2023, from https://www.vox.com/recode/2019/8/15/20806384/social-media-hate-speech-bias-black-african-american-facebook-twitter

Global ecommerce: Stats and trends to watch (2023). Shopify Plus. (n.d.). Retrieved March 3, 2023, from https://www.shopify.com/in/enterprise/global-ecommerce-statistics

Gupta, P. (2022, December 5). Internet sensation CHATGPT crosses 1 million users in 5 days. Entrepreneur. Retrieved March 3, 2023, from https://www.entrepreneur.com/en-in/news-and-trends/internet-sensation-chatgpt-crosses-1-million-users-in-5-days/440390

Göke, S., Staight, K., & Vrijen, R. (2022, June 7). Scaling AI in the sector that enables it: Lessons for semiconductor-device makers. McKinsey & Company. Retrieved March 3, 2023, from https://www.mckinsey.com/industries/semiconductors/our-insights/scaling-ai-in-the-sector-that-enables-it-lessons-for-semiconductor-device-makers

HMMJ: Horizons Marijuana Life Sciences index ETF overview. MarketWatch. (n.d.). Retrieved March 3, 2023, from https://www.marketwatch.com/investing/fund/hmmj?countrycode=ca

Harford, T. (2020, March 4). Was tulip mania really the first great financial bubble? BBC News. Retrieved March 3, 2023, from https://www.bbc.com/news/business-51311368

Hayes, A. (2023, January 18). Tulipmania: About the Dutch Tulip Bulb Market Bubble. Investopedia. Retrieved March 3, 2023, from https://www.investopedia.com/terms/d/dutch_tulip_bulb_market_bubble.asp

How ai trading technology works for stock investors. Built In. (n.d.). Retrieved March 3, 2023, from https://builtin.com/artificial-intelligence/ai-trading-stock-market-tech

Hulbert, M. (2023, February 15). How AI can help us become better investors. Barron's. Retrieved March 3, 2023, from https://www.barrons.com/articles/stock-market-s-p-500-investing-ai-technology-478fd9bf

IBM Global AI Adoption Index 2022. IBM. (2022). Retrieved March 3, 2023, from https://www.ibm.com/watson/resources/ai-adoption

Iacurci, G. (2023, January 12). Here's the inflation breakdown for December 2022 - in one chart. CNBC. Retrieved March 3, 2023, from https://www.cnbc.com/2023/01/12/heres-the-inflation-breakdown-for-december-2022-in-one-chart.html#:~:text=While%20on%20the%20decline%2C%20the,at%209.1%25%20in%20June%202022.

Iea. (n.d.). Trends in electric light-duty vehicles – global EV outlook 2022 – analysis. IEA. Retrieved March 3, 2023, from https://www.iea.org/reports/global-ev-outlook-2022/trends-in-electric-light-duty-vehicles

Inflation rates in the United States of America. Worlddata.info. (n.d.). Retrieved March 3, 2023, from https://www.worlddata.info/america/usa/inflation-rates.php#:~:text=During%20the%20observation%20period%20from,year%20inflation%20rate%20was%206.4%25.

Jackson, A.-L. (2021, May 19). Blowing bubbles: What is a stock market bubble? Forbes. Retrieved March 3, 2023, from https://www.forbes.com/advisor/investing/stock-market-bubble/

Kahn, J. (2020, August 25). Can an a.i.-driven hedge fund beat the market? Fortune. Retrieved March 3, 2023, from https://fortune.com/2020/08/25/can-an-a-i-hedge-fund-beat-the-market/

Kenton, W. (2022, October 20). What is an economic bubble and how does it work, with examples. Investopedia. Retrieved March 3, 2023, from https://www.investopedia.com/terms/b/bubble.asp

Labbe, M., & Wigmore, I. (2023, January 20). What is narrow ai (weak ai)? Enterprise AI. Retrieved March 2, 2023, from https://www.techtarget.com/searchenterpriseai/definition/narrow-AI-weak-AI

Lancôme creates groundbreaking AI beauty device to help people with disabilities apply makeup. Flipboard. (n.d.). Retrieved March 3, 2023, from https://flipboard.com/topic/disability/lanc-me-creates-groundbreaking-ai-beauty-device-to-help-people-with-disabilities/a-tIpPQHsdTCmVLT4zs0pt-w%3Aa%3A1952322242-fb62a26596%2Fco.uk

Lauret, J. (2019, August 16). Amazon's sexist AI recruiting tool: How did it go so wrong? Medium. Retrieved March 3, 2023, from https://becominghuman.ai/amazons-sexist-ai-recruiting-tool-how-did-it-go-so-wrong-e3d14816d98e

Lynch, D. J. (2022, February 7). Inflation has fed critics pointing to spike in money supply. The Washington Post. Retrieved March 3, 2023, from https://www.washingtonpost.com/business/2022/02/06/federal-reserve-inflation-money-supply/

MarketWatch. (2023, February 16). Nestle 2022 profit falls short of expectations; sets out guidance -- update. MarketWatch. Retrieved March 3, 2023, from https://www.marketwatch.com/story/nestle-2022-profit-falls-short-of-expectations-sets-out-guidance-update-877b7c3e

Marticio, D. (2022, January 15). What was the dotcom bubble? The Balance. Retrieved March 3, 2023, from https://www.thebalancemoney.com/what-was-the-dotcom-bubble-5209336

McCullough, B. (2018, December 4). A revealing look at the dot-com bubble of 2000 - and how it shapes our lives Today. ideas.ted.com. Retrieved March 3, 2023, from https://ideas.ted.com/an-eye-opening-look-at-the-dot-com-bubble-of-2000-and-how-it-shapes-our-lives-today/

Meyer, R. (2015, October 26). How did Hurricane Patricia get so strong so fast? The Atlantic. Retrieved March 3, 2023, from https://www.theatlantic.com/science/archive/2015/10/how-did-hurricane-patricia-intensify-so-fast/412246/

Mkdigiworld. (n.d.). Market makers survey reveals widespread adoption of AI in hedge fund industry for 2023. Newsfile. Retrieved March 3, 2023, from https://www.newsfilecorp.com/release/151760/Market-Makers-Survey-Reveals-Widespread-Adoption-of-AI-in-Hedge-Fund-Industry-for-2023

Monday, N. 11, & Law, M. (n.d.). Moore's law, part 1: Brief history of Moore's law and current State. Moore's Law, Part 1: Brief history of Moore's Law and current state – Google AI Blog. Retrieved March 3, 2023, from https://ai.googleblog.com/2013/11/moores-law-part-1-brief-history-of.html

Mullaney, T. (2022, August 11). The inflation argument that predicts another good decade for technology investing. CNBC. Retrieved March 3, 2023, from https://www.cnbc.com/2022/08/11/the-inflation-argument-calling-another-good-decade-for-tech-investing.html

Murphy, C. (2023, March 1). It inflation: where it is headed, and what to do about it. IDC Blog. Retrieved March 3, 2023, from https://blogs.idc.com/2022/06/08/it-inflation-where-it-is-headed-and-what-to-do-about-it/

New AI regulations are coming. is your organization ready? Harvard Business Review. (2021, May 3). Retrieved March 3, 2023, from https://hbr.org/2021/04/new-ai-regulations-are-coming-is-your-organization-ready

Odlyzko, A. (2020, July 1). Isaac Newton and the perils of the Financial South Sea. Physics Today. Retrieved March 3, 2023, from https://physicstoday.scitation.org/doi/10.1063/PT.3.4521#:~:text=His%20investments%20were%20primarily%20in,just%20over%20%C2%A330%20000.

Paul, H. (2022, September 13). 300 years since the South Sea bubble: The real story behind the iconic financial crash.

Pictet Asset Management. (2016, February 1). What are megatrends? Pictet Asset Management. Retrieved March 3, 2023, from https://am.pictet/en/globalwebsite/mega/megatrends-shaping-all-our-futures

Plc, G. D. (n.d.). Defense stocks rally amid russia-ukraine war. GlobalData. Retrieved March 3, 2023, from https://www.globaldata.com/data-insights/aerospace-and-defence/defense-stocks-rally-amid-russia-ukraine-war/

Popli, N. (2022, December 14). He made a children's book using AI. artists are not happy. Time. Retrieved March 3, 2023, from https://time.com/6240569/ai-childrens-book-alice-and-sparkle-artists-unhappy/

Press, S. F. X. Z. (2023, January 17). EVs made up 10% of all new cars sold last year. The Wall Street Journal. Retrieved March 3, 2023, from https://www.wsj.com/articles/evs-made-up-10-of-all-new-cars-sold-last-year-11673818385

PricewaterhouseCoopers. (n.d.). PWC's Global Artificial Intelligence Study: Sizing the prize. PwC. Retrieved March 2, 2023, from https://www.pwc.com/gx/en/issues/data-and-analytics/publications/artificial-intelligence-study.html

PricewaterhouseCoopers. (n.d.). PWC's Global Artificial Intelligence Study: Sizing the prize. PwC. Retrieved March 3, 2023, from https://www.pwc.com/gx/en/issues/data-and-analytics/publications/

artificial-intelligence-study.html

Roose, K. (2022, December 5). The brilliance and weirdness of chatgpt. The New York Times. Retrieved March 3, 2023, from https://www.nytimes.com/2022/12/05/technology/chatgpt-ai-twitter.html

Segal, T. (2022, July 8). 5 stages of a bubble. Investopedia. Retrieved March 3, 2023, from https://www.investopedia.com/articles/stocks/10/5-steps-of-a-bubble.asp#:~:text=The%20five%20steps%20in%20the,profit%2Dtaking%2C%20and%20panic.

Serafeim Loukas, P. D. (2023, February 8). What is machine learning: A short note on supervised, unsupervised, semi-supervised and... Medium. Retrieved March 2, 2023, from https://towardsdatascience.com/what-is-machine-learning-a-short-note-on-supervised-unsupervised-semi-supervised-and-aed1573ae9bb

Seth, S. (2022, December 22). Basics of Algorithmic Trading: Concepts and examples. Investopedia. Retrieved March 3, 2023, from https://www.investopedia.com/articles/active-trading/101014/basics-algorithmic-trading-concepts-and-examples.asp

Sga. (n.d.). Algorithmic trading accounts for nearly 60-73 of US equity trading. Retrieved March 3, 2023, from https://us.sganalytics.com/blog/algorithmic-trading-accounts-for-nearly-60-73-of-all-us-equity-trading-data-analytics-in-stock-market/

Skillings, J. (2007, September 14). Apple: 1 million iPhones sold. CNET. Retrieved March 3, 2023, from https://www.cnet.com/culture/apple-1-million-iphones-sold/

Srivastava, P. (2023, February 16). Top 12 B2C e-commerce websites dominating the Indian market. StartupTalky. Retrieved March 3, 2023, from https://startuptalky.com/top-b2c-ecommerce-websites-india/#:~:text=In%20fact%2C%20India%20is%20ranked,of%20%2416.6%20trillion%20by%202022.

Stewart, D., Lee, P., Bucaille, A., & Crossan, G. (2021, November 30). Ais wide shut: Ai regulation gets (even more) serious. Deloitte Insights. Retrieved March 3, 2023, from https://www2.deloitte.com/xe/en/insights/industry/technology/technology-media-and-telecom-predictions/2022/ai-regulation-trends.html

Taylor, P. (2023, January 18). Forecast number of Mobile Users Worldwide 2020-2025. Statista. Retrieved March 3, 2023, from https://www.statista.com/statistics/218984/number-of-global-mobile-users-since-2010/ https://www.counterpointresearch.com/global-smartphone-share/

Tech enters an era of inflation. Canalys Insights. (n.d.). Retrieved March 3, 2023, from https://canalys.com/insights/Tech-enters-an-era-of-inflation

Technology adoption curve: 5 stages of adoption. The Whatfix Blog | Drive Digital Adoption. (2023, February 24). Retrieved March 3, 2023, from https://whatfix.com/blog/technology-adoption-curve/

The Conversation. Retrieved March 3, 2023, from https://theconversation.com/300-years-since-the-south-sea-bubble-the-real-story-behind-the-iconic-financial-crash-143861

The United States Government. (2021, November 30). Historical parallels to today's inflationary episode. The White House. Retrieved March 3, 2023, from https://www.whitehouse.gov/cea/written-materials/2021/07/06/historical-parallels-to-todays-inflationary-episode/

Thomas Ross and Stevenson Smith. Computer Timeline. (n.d.). Retrieved March 2, 2023, from http://www.computer-timeline.com/timeline/thomas-ross-and-stevenson-smith/

Understanding the proposed EU AI act. Deloitte. (n.d.). Retrieved March 3, 2023, from https://www.deloitte.com/global/en/services/audit/perspectives/understanding-the-proposed-eu-ai-act.html

United States fed funds RATE2023 data - 1971-2022 historical - 2024 forecast. United States Fed Funds Rate - 2023 Data - 1971-2022 Historical - 2024 Forecast. (n.d.). Retrieved March 3, 2023, from https://tradingeconomics.com/united-states/interest-rate

What is an FPGA? field programmable gate array. Xilinx. (n.d.). Retrieved March 3, 2023, from https://www.xilinx.com/products/silicon-devices/fpga/what-is-an-fpga.html

What is strong AI? IBM. (n.d.). Retrieved March 2, 2023, from https://www.ibm.com/in-en/topics/strong-ai

What was the dot-com bubble & why did it burst? - thestreet. (n.d.). Retrieved March 3, 2023, from https://www.thestreet.com/dictionary/d/dot-com-bubble-and-burst

Witkowski, W. (2023, March 1). Apple, Samsung outlook grows darker as another smartphone decline is expected in 2023. MarketWatch. Retrieved March 3, 2023, from https://www.marketwatch.com/story/apple-samsung-forecast-grows-darker-as-another-smartphone-decline-is-expected-in-2023-ba4b637c

Writer, S. (2022, October 7). IPhone 14 teardown reveals parts 20% costlier than previous model. Nikkei Asia. Retrieved March 3, 2023, from https://asia.nikkei.com/Business/Technology/iPhone-14-teardown-reveals-parts-20-costlier-than-previous-model

You'll never guess what the first thing ever sold on the internet was. (2015, November). Retrieved March 3, 2023, from https://www.fastcompany.com/3054025/youll-never-guess-what-the-first-thing-ever-sold-on-the-internet-was

Zewe, A. | MIT News Office. (2022, January). Demystifying machine-learning systems. MIT News | Massachusetts Institute of Technology. Retrieved March 2, 2023, from https://news.mit.edu/2022/explainable-machine-learning-0127

Printed in Dunstable, United Kingdom

72263976R00099